CYCLING ANATOMY

Shannon Sovndal, MD

Human Kinetics

Library of Congress Cataloging-in-Publication Data

Sovndal, Shannon, 1970-
    Cycling anatomy / Shannon Sovndal.
      p. cm.
    ISBN-13: 978-0-7360-7587-9 (soft cover)
    ISBN-10: 0-7360-7587-9 (soft cover)
    1. Cycling--Training. 2. Cycling--Training--Charts, diagrams, etc. 3. Cycling--Physiological aspects. I. Title.
    GV1048.S68 2009
    796.6--dc22

                                   2008041616

ISBN-10: 0-7360-7587-9 (print)
ISBN-13: 978-0-7360-7587-9 (print)
ISBN-10: 0-7360-8525-4 (Adobe PDF)
ISBN-13: 978-0-7360-8525-0 (Adobe PDF)

This publication is written and published to provide accurate and authoritative information relevant to the subject matter presented. It is published and sold with the understanding that the author and publisher are not engaged in rendering legal, medical, or other professional services by reason of their authorship or publication of this work. If medical or other expert assistance is required, the services of a competent professional person should be sought.

Acquisitions Editor: Tom Heine; **Developmental Editor:** Leigh Keylock; **Assistant Editor:** Laura Podeschi; **Copyeditor:** Patrick Connolly; **Proofreader:** Kathy Bennett; **Permission Manager:** Martha Gullo; **Graphic Designer:** Fred Starbird; **Graphic Artist:** Francine Hamerski; **Cover Designer:** Keith Blomberg; **Photographer (for illustration references):** Neil Bernstein; **Photo Asset Manager:** Laura Fitch; **Visual Production Assistant:** Joyce Brumfield; **Art Manager:** Kelly Hendren; **Associate Art Manager:** Alan L. Wilborn; **Illustrator (cover):** Jennifer Gibas; **Illustrators (interior):** Jennifer Gibas and Andrew Recher; **Printer:** United Graphics

Human Kinetics books are available at special discounts for bulk purchase. Special editions or book excerpts can also be created to specification. For details, contact the Special Sales Manager at Human Kinetics.

Printed in the United States of America   10 9 8 7 6 5

The paper in this book is certified under a sustainable forestry program.

Human Kinetics
Web site: www.HumanKinetics.com

United States: Human Kinetics
P.O. Box 5076
Champaign, IL 61825-5076
800-747-4457
e-mail: humank@hkusa.com

Canada: Human Kinetics
475 Devonshire Road, Unit 100
Windsor, ON N8Y 2L5
800-465-7301 (in Canada only)
e-mail: info@hkcanada.com

Europe: Human Kinetics
107 Bradford Road
Stanningley
Leeds LS28 6AT, United Kingdom
+44 (0)113 255 5665
e-mail: hk@hkeurope.com

Australia: Human Kinetics
57A Price Avenue
Lower Mitcham, South Australia 5062
08 8372 0999
e-mail: info@hkaustralia.com

New Zealand: Human Kinetics
P.O. Box 80
Torrens Park, South Australia 5062
0800 222 062
e-mail: info@hknewzealand.com

To my sister, Melissa

CONTENTS

FOREWORD

There's nothing better than feeling your fitness peak at just the right moment. Flying over a mountain pass in the Pyrenees or blasting through the finish line during a time trial makes all the work in the gym and on the road worthwhile. All cyclists know that they need to train on their bikes to go fast. But what many fail to realize is that the entire body—all the muscle groups, not just the legs—works to propel the bike.

I have been friends with Shannon Sovndal for quite a while. Throughout that time he has seen me go through the biggest injuries and setbacks of my career. I have depended on Shannon as a friend, a training partner, and, as of last year, my team doctor. Through our many discussions he has helped me realize that strength is the foundation of my cycling health and success. Many of my problems have come from rushing back into racing before I adequately rehabilitated from injury. My back, hips, and shoulders have given me problems because they weren't properly conditioned for my high training load.

I remember going to the gym with Shannon and being impressed by his knowledge of anatomy and physiology. I was humbled as he showed me the exercises that I should be doing. Now, after many years of dragging my feet to the weight room, I see the importance of this component of my training, and I embrace it.

I have significantly changed my body through physical therapy and strength training, and my race results have shown the benefits. I am now a firm believer in proper and consistent gym work. Not only do I strength train during the off-season, but I also regularly go to the gym throughout the entire year for maintenance. This is a bit different from the old-school approach, but it has clearly been beneficial for me.

My conditioning has also helped me feel more healthy and strong in everday tasks. The days of avoiding picking up a suitcase or taking part in any other activity out of fear of getting hurt are gone. Strength conditioning is something that I will continue to pursue for the rest of my active life.

In *Cycling Anatomy,* Shannon Sovndal addresses the issue of conditioning each muscle group to give you the best performance on the road. This book will help you meet your true cycling potential. The exercises were chosen to match the needs of cyclists. Try these out in your workouts, and you'll see improvements in your performance on the bike.

Christian Vande Velde
Professional road cyclist

CHAPTER 1

THE CYCLIST IN MOTION

In cycling, as in any other athletic endeavor, the athlete's body must have a strong, solid base. This is the key to reaching top performance, avoiding injury, and achieving longevity in the sport. For you to obtain your peak performance, all your systems must be operating in concert and as a single coordinated unit. Many cyclists fall into the trap of thinking that cycling is all about the legs. Unfortunately, it is not that simple. Your legs, hips, and buttocks do generate the majority of your cycling power, but to stabilize the lower half of your body, you need to have a strong abdomen, back, and upper body. All sections of your body must work together to stabilize the bike and deliver maximum power to the pedals.

This book explains the anatomy of cycling through various training exercises. With this knowledge base you will have better focus during your workouts. You will be able to design your program based on the understanding that complete balance and strength are the key to successful and injury-free riding. The illustrations and descriptions in each chapter will show you how each exercise applies to cycling. You'll be able to take what you've trained in the gym and directly apply it to your training on the road. Focusing your mind on the cycling aspect of the workout will enable you to make the best use of your time while working out in the gym. As a result, you will get more benefits out of each exercise.

This book emphasizes the need to train your entire body. No single chapter in the book is more important than any other. Cycling is a full-body activity. This will become clear as you read the anatomic description of the cyclist in motion. Each area of the body plays a vital role in distributing your power to the pedals, controlling your bicycle, and preventing injury. If you lack training in a particular area of your body, the entire system falls out of alignment. This will not only cause a degradation in performance, but may also result in pain or injury.

Muscle Form and Function in Cycling

The cyclist in motion is amazing. So many aspects of human physiology come into play when you ride a bicycle. Your cerebral cortex supplies the motivation and plan of attack when you climb onto your bike. You effortlessly maintain the stability and direction of your bicycle through the unconscious balance and coordination provided by your cerebellum. Your heart, lungs, and vascular system supply much-needed oxygen to the mitochondria of your muscles. Through both aerobic and anaerobic energy conversion, your muscles contract and perform a huge amount of work. All this work creates heat, and your skin and respirations help keep the temperature well regulated. Your skeletal system supplies the structural foundation of the entire system. Nearly every physiologic system needs to function in coordination to allow you to complete your bike ride. If you stop and think it through, you realize that it's truly remarkable!

Although each of these systems can be further broken down and exhaustively explained, *Cycling Anatomy* focuses on describing how to train the various muscles used while riding a bike. To help you understand why weight training improves performance, let's begin with a brief explanation of muscle physiology. Once you understand how a muscle works, you'll also understand the optimal muscle position and, hence, the importance of proper form during your exercises.

The fundamental functional unit of the skeletal muscle is called the motor unit. It is composed of a single motor nerve (neuron) and all the muscle fibers it innervates. Each muscle fiber breaks down into numerous ropelike myofibrils that are bundled together (see figure 1.1). By activating more or fewer motor units, the muscle generates a gradation of tension. *Graded* muscle activity refers to this variable tension generation. The frequency at which the nerve activates the motor unit also contributes to muscle tension. The most notable example of this is tetanus, which occurs when the nerve fires so fast that there is no time for relaxation of the muscle. When you decide to lift a particular weight in the gym, your brain controls both the number of motor nerves fired and the rate at which the firing occurs. The brain is stunning in its ability to estimate the needed effort. Only rarely do you realize your brain made a miscalculation. For example, if you pick up a milk carton that you think is full but is actually empty, you will rapidly lift the carton far beyond the spot you intended. In this situation, your mind makes an estimation that is proved wrong, and a poorly coordinated movement results.

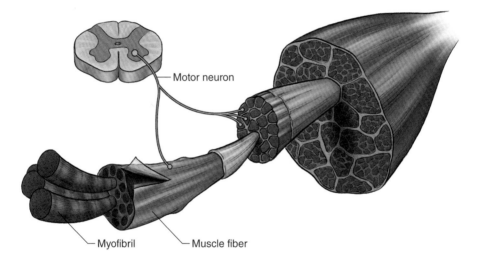

Figure 1.1   Details of a muscle fiber.
Adapted, by permission, from National Strength and Conditioning Association, 2008, *Essentials of strength and conditioning*, 3rd ed. (Champaign, IL: Human Kinetics), 5.

Composed of actin filaments and myosin filaments, muscle fibers work like a ratchet system. Figure 1.2 shows the functional structure of a muscle. The action of a muscle fiber can be compared to a rock climber on a rope. In this analogy, the rope represents muscle actin, and the climber represents muscle myosin. Just as a climber pulls himself up with his arms, the myosin pulls itself along the actin. Imagine the climber clinging to a rope. To move upward, he locks his legs, outstretches his arms, and pulls. Repeatedly, myosin climbs the actin. As the myosin moves along, the muscle fiber shortens, or contracts. This creates tension and allows the muscle to perform work.

Each muscle has an optimal resting length. This optimal length represents the perfect compromise between having a large number of cross-linked actin and myosin while still leaving enough "spare rope" for the myosin to climb up. Overstretching or understretching wastes the full energy potential of the muscle. This is why a proper fit on your bicycle is so important. If your seat is too low, the muscles won't be stretched to the optimal length; if your seat is too high, the muscles may be overstretched.

Your position while lifting weights is just as important as your position on the bike. To ensure that you optimally work your muscles while in the gym, you need to follow the form laid out in this book for each exercise. Weightlifters often forgo proper form in order to increase the amount of weight lifted. This is counterproductive. The amount of weight takes second priority to the necessity of doing the exercise correctly. This book shows you the proper technique for effectively working the various muscle groups. Pictures are worth a thousand words, and the many illustrations in the book will guide you by demonstrating ideal form and subsequent muscle fiber position. Following these images will enable you to get the most out of your workout.

Figure 1.3 shows proper cycling position on a road bike. Note that there are five points of contact with the bicycle (legs, buttocks, and arms). In addition, most major muscle groups will be engaged during the cycling motion. Individual chapters of this book will focus on the anatomy of various body sections. But before we focus on particular exercises and individual areas of the body, let's look at a brief overview of the anatomy of the cyclist in motion.

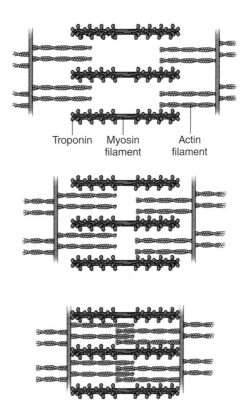

Figure 1.2 Actin and myosin filaments in the muscle fiber work like a ratchet system. Adapted, by permission, from National Strength and Conditioning Association, 2008, *Essentials of strength and conditioning,* 3rd ed. (Champaign, IL: Human Kinetics), 7.

If you need help properly fitting your bicycle, you can find information in *Fitness Cycling* (Human Kinetics, 2006). You can also have a professional bike fit done. Check your local bicycle shops and clubs for recommendations on the best fitting services.

Because the cranks on a bike extend 180 degrees in opposite directions, one of the cyclist's legs will be extended when the other leg is flexed. This allows the flexor muscles on one leg to work at the same time that extensors are firing on the opposite side. With each rhythmic turn of the crank, the legs will cycle through all the various muscle groups. This is why cycling is a great exercise and why the pedal stroke is such an efficient means of propulsion. In proper form, you should have only a slight bend at the knee when your leg is in the 6 o'clock position. This stretches the hamstring to the ideal length and prepares for optimal firing during the upward pedal stroke. At the same time, the opposite pedal is at the 12 o'clock position, causing your thigh to be nearly parallel with the ground. This optimizes the gluteus maximus for maximal power output during the downward stroke and the quadriceps for a strong kick as your foot rounds the top of your pedaling motion.

As you rotate through the pedal stroke, your ankle will allow your foot to smoothly transition from the knee-flexed position to the knee-extended position. Just as the flexors and extensors of your upper leg alternate as they travel in the pedaling circle, your calf and

Figure 1.3 Proper cycling position.

lower leg muscles will add to the power curve during most of the pedaling motion. The calf and lower leg muscles will also help stabilize the ankle and foot. As discussed earlier, the maximum energy potential (tension) of the muscle depends on the ideal amount of overlapping actin and myosin. Proper seat height plays a key role in establishing this proper muscle position. If you've ever tried to ride a kid's bike with a low seat, you probably have a good idea of how poorly your muscles perform when they are not positioned correctly.

Because of the basic bent-over position of the rider on a bike, a strong and healthy back is crucial to cycling performance and enjoyment. That doesn't mean you shouldn't ride if you've ever had back problems. Rather, it means that you'll need to strengthen and care for your back if you want to have a long cycling career. The erector spinae, latissimus dorsi, and trapezius muscles support the spine as you lean forward on the bike. When riding in the handlebar drops, these muscles will help flatten your back, providing better aerodynamics. Riding also stresses your neck. Both the splenius and the trapezius help keep your eyes on the road by extending your neck. Again, because of the strain on all these muscles, proper conditioning of your back is a necessity for healthy and pain-free riding.

The rectus abdominis, transversus abdominis, and abdominal obliques (internal and external) provide anterior and lateral support to the torso, countering the well-developed muscles of the back. If either the back, anterior, or lateral muscles are weak compared to the others, you'll experience poor spinal alignment, unnecessary spinal stress, and pain. Back pain may have nothing to do with malfunctioning or weak back muscles. It may, in fact, be caused by a lack of conditioning of the abdominal muscles. This is an excellent example of why you need to work on strengthening the entire system rather than a few selected parts of the whole.

Your arms contact the bike for both control and power delivery. While you are holding the handlebars, each arm should maintain a slight bend at the elbow. As you pedal, the flexors and extensors in your arm will alternate from contraction to relaxation. The biceps, triceps, and forearm muscles all work in unison to stabilize your torso via the shoulder joint. Because of your riding position, your shoulder is constantly under pressure. Numerous muscle groups—including the rhomboid, rotator cuff, and deltoid—help maintain proper stability and position.

Your chest muscles support and balance the musculature of your back and shoulders. The pectoralis major and minor allow you to lean forward on the bike and move the handlebars from side to side while climbing. Notice that the form of a rider with his hands in the handlebar drops mimics the position for push-ups or the bench press.

From this brief overview of the anatomy of the cyclist, it is clear that cycling involves the entire body. The various exercises in this book will help you optimize your riding through complete-body training. No area of the body is less important than any other area, so you should be sure not to bypass any chapters. Remember, balance and symmetry are the keys to proper form—and proper form is required for you to gain power and to limit the risk of injury.

The exercises in each chapter will not only improve your strength but will also improve your flexibility. Studies have shown that good flexibility prevents injury and optimizes power output. Your ability to meet the cardiorespiratory demands of cycling will also be improved by work in the gym. During your gym workouts, vascular structures that distribute blood to the muscles will be enhanced, and this will ultimately pay dividends with oxygen delivery to the muscles during high-demand workouts.

Finally, resistance training also has health benefits for your bones. Cycling allows the rider to exercise without unduly stressing the joints. However, this benefit also has a downside. In any type of training, stress develops strength. Because of the smooth pedaling motion, very little stress occurs at the bone. Athletes who only participate in cycling have an increased risk of osteoporosis. This is another reason why weight training is crucial for avid cyclists. Time spent in the gym will help prevent weak and injury-prone bones. Resistance training enhances bone mineralization, making your bony architecture stronger. So when you're in the gym training, you're gaining not only fitness but also long-term health benefits.

Strength Training Principles and Recommendations

Before you hit the gym, you need to understand a couple of training principles. The general adaptation syndrome (GAS) provides the fundamental construct for weight training. The GAS is made up of three phases: alarm reaction, adaptation, and exhaustion. The human body likes to maintain homeostasis. It constantly works to resist change and remain at rest. Every time the body experiences a new stress—such as a longer-than-normal bike ride or weightlifting—the body becomes "alarmed." The stressor disturbs the natural homeostasis and moves the body out of its comfort zone. Phase 2 occurs when the body tries to mitigate the stress by adapting to it. The body will reach a new, higher level of homeostasis as a result of the adaptation. Ideally, as you train, you'll repeat phases 1 and 2 to continually improve your level of strength and fitness. If you overdo it, however, you may overwhelm your body's adaptive abilities. This will cause you to reach the third phase of the GAS: exhaustion. You'll find that your training is a fine balance of stress and recovery. Be sure to allow yourself adequate rest between workouts. Remember, adaptation and conditioning come while you are resting and recovering, not while you are working out.

Periodization is another key training concept that goes hand in hand with the GAS. All training should be based on a well-planned, systematic, and stepwise approach that involves training cycles being built one on top of the other. This hierarchical structure continually builds on previous gains while giving the body time to adapt and condition. A good periodization program will enable you to avoid overtraining and to continually improve your fitness level. Think of the periodization program as the big picture of your training. The program will help you work toward particular periods when you want peak fitness. The various training periods can vary in length, but they will usually range between two and four weeks. Thus, as you use this book to plan your various workouts, you should choose different exercises during each block in an effort to continually "alarm" your system. This is the best way to improve your strength and conditioning.

Scientific studies have shown that strength training improves endurance performance. It is not enough for you to merely go put miles on your bike. If you truly want to reach your potential, you'll also need to use a weight training program. Resistance training enhances strength, blood flow, and oxygen delivery to the muscles; all these attributes will improve your cycling performance.

It is not within the scope of this book to provide complete workout programs. Rather, the goal is to show the cyclist proper weight training exercises and correct lifting techniques. Each chapter offers a variety of exercises, and during the course of your training, you should vary the exercises that you choose to use from each chapter. To help you get the most out of your time in the gym, you should follow these general rules for training:

• **Work your entire body.** As mentioned earlier, focusing only on your legs and buttocks can result in instability and possible injury. For you to obtain peak performance, your entire body must be in equilibrium. You should choose a program that includes exercises from each chapter of this book. This will help ensure that your program covers all the muscles involved in cycling. You'll find that different exercises stress different things, such as flexibility, accessory muscles, primary muscles, or stability. For each area of your body (arms, trunk, back, buttocks, legs), you should pick a few exercises to use during each training period. I also recommend that you cover multiple body parts during each visit to the gym. This is different from pure bodybuilding programs. Those programs often involve working only certain body parts during each visit, and they also require the person to visit the gym five or six times per week. As a cyclist, you need to continue with your cardiorespiratory training; therefore, you should perform resistance training no more than three days a week. The other days should be spent riding your bike!

• **Remember that consistency is the key to success.** Try to set a program and stick with it. Strength and conditioning are all about building on your previous gains and workouts. Working out two or three times per week will improve your power output and fitness. If you have limited time, try to schedule at least one day per week in the gym in order to maintain previous gains. Deconditioning is one of your worst enemies. If you fail to visit the gym for weeks at a time, you will lose previous training benefits. Unfortunately, loss occurs much more rapidly than the gains, so you will find yourself fighting an uphill battle if you inconsistently visit the gym.

• **Vary your workout program.** Every two to four weeks, you should set up a new training program in order to keep your body under stress. Adaptation is the key! Your body improves its strength and fitness through adaptation. (A more thorough explanation can be found in *Fitness Cycling.*) Adaptation is your body's response to a given stress. Your job is to keep your body surprised by the workout so that you get the most adaptation possible. This book provides many exercises so you'll have plenty of choices to keep your workout fresh and new.

THE CYCLIST IN MOTION

- **Vary the exercises within your program.** Obviously, you should not plan on doing every exercise in the book when you go to the gym. (That would take forever and likely cause injury!) During each training block, you should choose a group of exercises from each chapter so that you are working your whole body. You should also try to use a combination of free weights, machines, and the stability ball. By training with a wide variety of exercises, not only will you keep your body stressed, but you'll also keep your mind interested in going to the gym. When practical, you can also exercise your arms or legs individually and in tandem. This will ensure that your weak side isn't being supported by your strong side.

- **Mimic your cycling position.** While doing weight training exercises, try to mirror your position on the bike. For example, when doing calf raises, position your feet the same way your cycling shoes interact with the pedals. This will help focus the gains you achieve so that they can be directly applied when you are on the bike. Don't go overboard with this, however. Remember that well-rounded strength will help stabilize joints and prevent injury.

- **Visualize riding your bicycle.** While lifting in the gym, you can enhance your workout by thinking about the ways the exercise relates to riding. For example, when performing a squat, think of sprinting on your bicycle. As you strain to stand upright with the barbell, imagine powering the cranks downward through your pedaling motion. With the final repetition, see yourself nipping your opponent at the line for the win! The information for each exercise includes a Cycling Focus section that shows how the exercise relates to your position on the bike. However, you shouldn't limit yourself to what is contained in this section. If you can feel or visualize other applicable cycling positions and situations, then your training will only be further enhanced. Don't underestimate the value of visualization. Most professional athletes incorporate frequent visualization in their training regimen.

Types of Weight Training Workouts

Weight training can be done using various types of workouts. A well-rounded program touches on all the various workout strategies at some point. As previously discussed, for a given training block, you can focus on one specific type of workout. During subsequent training blocks, change the type of training so that you get the most adaptation possible. For example, if you do circuit training during your first block, your second block should be something different, such as low weight–high repetitions. You can use the various types of training in any order that you like. However, keep in mind that it is better to work up to high weight–low repetitions in order to avoid injury from lifting heavier weights. Again, setting up specific workouts for your cycling goals is beyond the scope of this book. Mix and match the following types of workouts when creating your training program.

The key to success is efficient training—that is, getting the most out of your effort. Preplanning your workouts and creating a workable training program will greatly enhance your performance over the course of your training season.

- **Low weight–high repetitions.** This workout will help you achieve a sustained strength without substantially bulking up your muscle mass. This is good for cyclists because you'll want to build the most strength with the least amount of mass (that's what enables you to ride up hills the fastest!). This type of workout will also help develop your cardiorespiratory fitness and your ability to crank out longer periods of hard riding. During each set, you should be able to complete 10 to 15 repetitions.

- **High weight–low repetitions.** This workout will help you develop raw power and strength. Whether you need to surge on a steep climb or sprint for the finish, pure power will help you reach your goal. For this workout, the weight is the maximum amount you can lift 4 to 8 times. Generally, you should do 2 or 3 sets of each exercise. Although this type of workout does build more bulk, it is appropriate for cyclists at certain times. You will usually need someone to spot you during these exercises.

- **Circuit training.** This workout involves moving through numerous exercises without much rest in between the various sets. Generally, this type of workout covers the entire body, and your heart rate is elevated throughout the entire workout. Circuit training not only builds strength but also improves cardiorespiratory fitness. This will pay dividends when you spend time at your anaerobic threshold while training or racing.

- **Pyramid sets.** In this type of training, the weight or repetitions are either increased or decreased for each set during the workout. You should do 3 sets per exercise. For example, in the first set, you may do 10 repetitions. For the second set, you would increase the weight and do 8 repetitions. For the third set, you would increase the weight again and perform 6 repetitions. The workouts usually focus on developing raw power and strength.

- **Supersets.** These workouts consist of a single set that includes a large number of repetitions. As you begin to tire during the set, the weight is reduced so that you can continue the repetitions. A typical set will have 30 to 40 repetitions. These workouts are very tiring, and they help you develop sustained strength and power. At some point, every cyclist should include this type of workout in her gym training. You'll be amazed at the driving power you have on your bike after you finish a training cycle of supersets.

Warm-Up, Cool-Down, and Stretching

You must take good care of your body before, during, and after your workouts. When you arrive at the gym, you should do a 5- to 10-minute cardio warm-up. This could be done on a stationary bike or a treadmill. I prefer the rowing machine because it works all the muscles at the same time. Each chapter includes a brief description of a warm-up that focuses on the muscles discussed in that chapter. Note, though, that since you will be working all the muscle groups during each workout, you'll need to warm up in a way that covers all areas.

After you get the heart rate up and feel that the muscles are warm, you should take 5 minutes to stretch. You should hold each position for at least 30 seconds and remember not to bounce while stretching. During your workout, if you feel a muscle cramping or causing you pain at any time, take a few moments to assess the situation. If the discomfort continues, stop the workout and spend some time stretching the troubled area. Once finished with your workout, you should stretch again. This will enhance the benefits of the weight training you just completed. Studies have shown that a well-stretched muscle provides greater power output and performance when compared to a nonstretched muscle that is similarly conditioned.

Strength, flexibility, and cardiorespiratory fitness all play a role in your cycling success. Complete fitness comes when all three of these are optimized, so you need to balance your entire training program to accomplish this. Visiting the gym should be an integral part of your complete training program, and the gains made will definitely improve your conditioning on the bike.

Your arms provide two of the five contact points with your bike. Not only do they significantly contribute to your bike handling, but they also serve as a foundation and platform to stabilize your body while you are pedaling. A strong foundation in your upper extremities will serve you well. Think of being on your bike and climbing out of the saddle— you will throw your bike back and forth with your arms as your legs power the rotation of the cranks. Your arms also play a key role during sprints or climbs out of the saddle. When you see a photograph of a sprint finish in a cycling race, you can't help but notice the strain and muscle flexion in the riders' arms. Even when you are riding on the flats, your arms stabilize the rest of your body. They connect the bike to your shoulders, which in turn stabilize your chest, back, and trunk. Again, each body section contributes to the whole cyclist. While you perform the exercises in this book, you should use the information in the Cycling Focus section to mentally apply your workout to your cycling performance.

Skeletal Anatomy

The humerus is the sole bone of the upper arm. Proximally (closer to the origin), the humerus sits in the glenoid fossa to form the shoulder joint. Chapter 3 discusses this joint in detail. Distally (farther away from the origin), the humerus forms the upper half of the elbow. The lower arm, or forearm, is composed of two bones called the radius and ulna. These bones, combined with the humerus, come together to form the elbow joint. The olecranon process of the ulna is the round point of the elbow that you feel when you bend your arm. As a simple hinge joint, it moves in flexion and extension. Flexion reduces the angle of the joint and brings the forearm up to the upper arm. Extension increases the angle of the elbow joint and straightens the arm. The forearm also rotates back and forth in supination and pronation. Supination turns the palm up, and pronation turns the palm down. Both the radius and the ulna articulate with the bones of the hand to form the complex wrist joint.

Biceps

The biceps muscle (see figure 2.1 on page 10) is composed of two heads. The long head of the biceps originates in the shoulder joint at the glenoid. The short head originates at the protruding coracoid process. These two muscles combine to form the biceps tendon and aponeurosis (fibrous membrane that connects muscle to bone). The biceps tendon inserts just below the elbow joint onto the tuberosity of the medial (inside) portion of the radius. Activation of the biceps muscle causes flexion (bending) at the elbow joint. Because of its insertion site, the biceps also causes supination of the forearm (rotation of the forearm so that the palm faces up).

   Although the biceps is the most well known, there are two other flexors of the elbow. The brachialis muscle originates along the anterior lower half of the humerus, crossing the elbow joint to insert at the proximal end of the ulna. As the biceps muscle pulls up on the radius, the brachialis pulls up on the ulna, and they work together to forcefully flex the elbow. The brachioradialis muscle arises from the lower lateral (outside) portion of the humerus, courses down the entire forearm, and inserts at the radius just above the wrist joint.

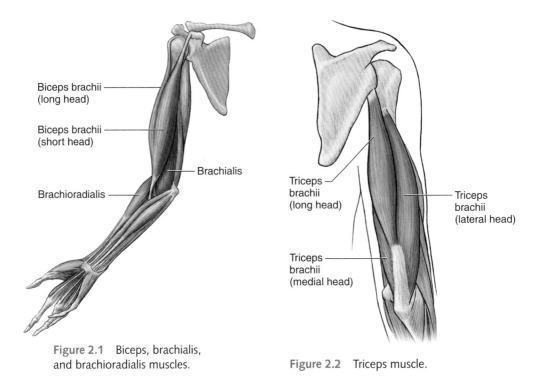

Figure 2.1 Biceps, brachialis, and brachioradialis muscles.

Figure 2.2 Triceps muscle.

The coracobrachialis is an often forgotten muscle of the upper arm. Its primary role is to adduct the humerus. Adduction moves the limb closer to the core, or sagittal plane. (Remember that you are "adding" your limb to the core by bringing it closer.) Like the biceps muscle, the coracobrachialis muscle originates at the coracoid process and inserts on the inside, middle portion of the humerus.

Triceps

As the name implies, the triceps muscle is composed of three heads: the long head, the medial head, and the lateral head (see figure 2.2). The long head of the triceps originates just under the glenoid cavity of the scapula. The medial head has the most extensive origin, running all along the medial and posterior aspect of the humerus. The lateral head originates along the upper posterior of the humerus. All three of these muscle heads fuse together to form the common triceps tendon that attaches to the olecranon process of the ulna. Whereas three muscles perform elbow flexion (biceps, brachialis, and brachioradialis), the triceps muscle is solely responsible for elbow extension (straightening the arm). If a fracture occurs that displaces the olecranon process, the triceps will cease to have a lever point to straighten the elbow. Unfortunately, this bone is broken somewhat frequently because it is the first point of contact when a person falls on his elbow. Surgical repair may be needed to facilitate full recovery.

Forearm

The forearm is an extremely intricate area of anatomy. Because there are so many move-ments of the wrist, hand, and fingers, a complicated array of muscles cram into this small location. For simplification, these muscles can be divided into the flexor group found on the palm side of the forearm and the extensor group found on the opposite side, or dorsal side, of the forearm (see figure 2.3). In addition to movement at the wrist and fingers, the two bones of the forearm can rotate as previously discussed. The supinator and biceps muscles supinate the forearm, turning the palm up. The pronator quadratus and the pronator teres muscles pronate the forearm, turning the palm down. Other muscles of the wrist and fingers can be divided as follows:

Wrist flexors: Flexor carpi radialis, palmaris longus, flexor carpi ulnaris

Finger flexors: Flexor digitorum superficialis, flexor digitorum profundus, flexor pollicis longus

Wrist extensors: Extensor carpi radialis longus, extensor carpi radialis brevis, extensor carpi ulnaris

Finger extensors: Extensor digitorum, extensor digitorum minimi, extensor indicis, extensor pollicis longus, extensor pollicis brevis

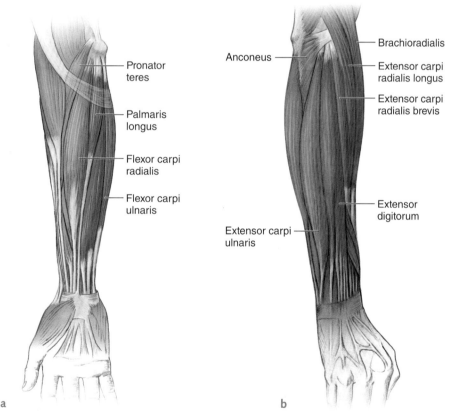

Figure 2.3   Forearm muscles: *(a)* flexors and *(b)* extensors.

Warm-Up and Stretching

Spend at least 10 minutes warming up before you start to lift. Make sure you emphasize your upper extremities. An elliptical machine with moving handles or a rowing machine can be used to effectively get the blood flowing to your arms. You can also try push-ups (with your knees on the ground), bar hangs, and arm rotations. Before lifting, you should also perform simple stretches of your biceps, triceps, forearm, and shoulder.

Standing Barbell Curl

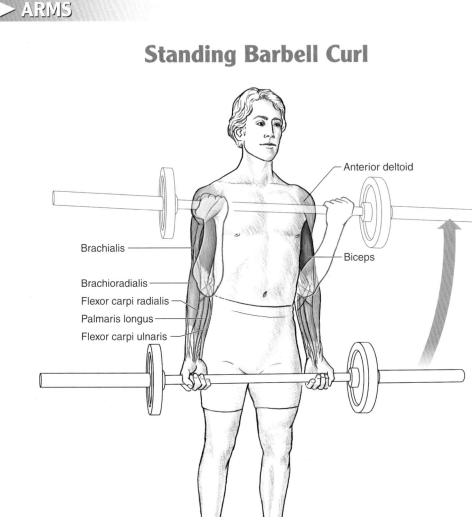

Anterior deltoid

Brachialis

Biceps

Brachioradialis

Flexor carpi radialis

Palmaris longus

Flexor carpi ulnaris

Execution

1. Stand with your feet shoulder-width apart and your knees slightly bent. With your arms extended down, hold the barbell using a shoulder-width underhand grip.
2. Keeping your elbows tight to your sides, curl the bar to your shoulders.
3. Lower the barbell until your arms are again in the extended position.

Muscles Involved

Primary: Biceps

Secondary: Brachialis, brachioradialis, anterior deltoid, forearm flexors

Cycling Focus

Once you start to climb on your bicycle and stand out of the saddle, you can't help but feel the support and effort of your arms. With every rotation of the pedals, you'll feel your arms stabilize the bicycle as it naturally moves from side to side. The input from your biceps helps counter the force from the driving leg. If you ever doubt the arms' contribution, try to take one of your hands off the handlebar while you're hammering up a hill (but don't crash!). As you perform the barbell curl, imagine yourself pulling up on the handlebar and powering down on the pedal with your leg. Position your arms handlebar-width apart to mimic your cycling position. To better isolate the

biceps, you should avoid rocking your torso during each repetition. Try standing on stability disks to enhance your lower extremity workout. The stability disks will train all the smaller stabilizing muscles of your lower extremities and torso. This will help you maintain form on the bicycle when you become fatigued.

⚠️ **SAFETY TIP** Keep your back straight and motionless during the exercise. Don't rock your body to aid in lifting the barbell. This movement can lead to back injury, and it also hinders the isolation workout of your arm muscles.

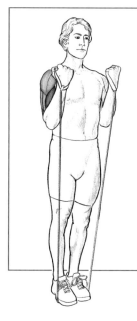

VARIATION

Resistance Band Curl

Perform the same motion as described for the barbell curl, but use a resistance band instead of a barbell. Hold the resistance band like a jump rope, and stand on the band. Keeping your elbows tight at your sides, bend your arms to bring your hands to your shoulders. Slowly return your hands to your sides. This is a great exercise to use when traveling because a band is easy to pack. The resistance band curl is also an excellent warm-up and stretching exercise.

Dumbbell Curl

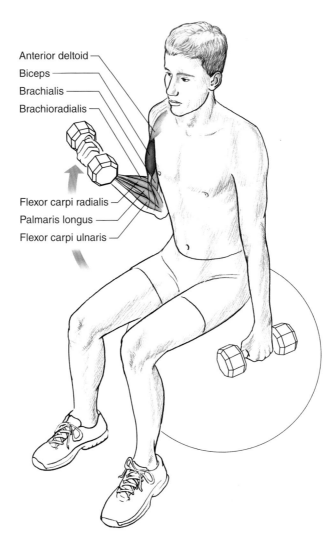

Anterior deltoid
Biceps
Brachialis
Brachioradialis

Flexor carpi radialis
Palmaris longus
Flexor carpi ulnaris

Execution

1. Sit on a stability ball or bench, and hold a pair of dumbbells. Your arms should be straight at your sides, and your thumbs should be forward.
2. Bring one dumbbell up to your shoulder on the same side (palm up).
3. Lower the dumbbell until your arm is back in the extended position, and then repeat on the opposite side.

Muscles Involved

Primary: Biceps

Secondary: Brachialis, brachioradialis, anterior deltoid, forearm flexors

Cycling Focus

Sprinting generates the highest power output by cyclists. To deliver maximal power while maintaining directional control, the cyclist must apply a strong counterforce on the handlebars. The dumbbell and isolation curl exercises help isolate the muscles used to pull up on the handlebars while sprinting. With each alternating curl, you should imagine the similar motion of rhythmically pulling up from side to side on your handlebars. While performing the curling motion, you should also focus on squeezing the bar. This will help train your forearm flexors and improve your grip strength for riding.

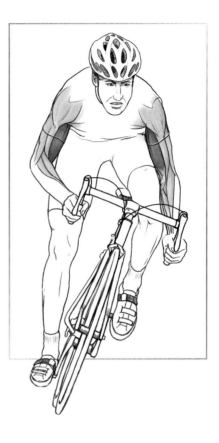

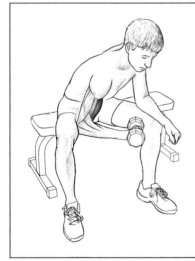

VARIATION

Isolation Curl

Sit on the edge of a bench or stability ball. Holding the dumbbell in one arm, extend at the elbow. Rest the back of your arm against your inner thigh. Curl the dumbbell to your shoulder and slowly return to the starting position. Maintain a motionless torso during the exercise. This exercise will help target the brachialis muscle.

Preacher Curl

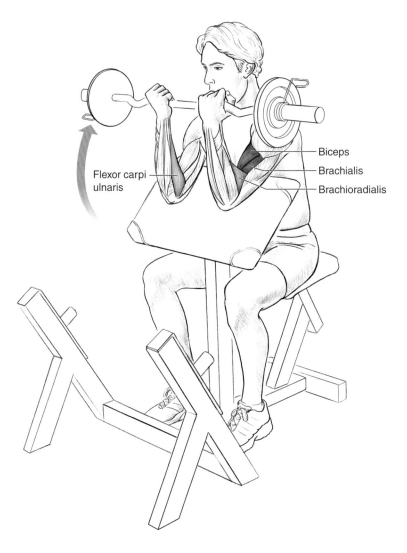

Flexor carpi ulnaris

Biceps

Brachialis

Brachioradialis

Execution

1. Holding an EZ bar or straight barbell, rest the back of your arms on the preacher bench; your elbows should be nearly straight.
2. Slowly bend your elbows and bring the bar toward your chin.
3. Return the weight to the starting position (arms extended).

Muscles Involved

Primary: Biceps, brachialis

Secondary: Brachioradialis, forearm flexors

Cycling Focus

I'll never forget the day Greg Lemond beat Sean Kelly in the final sprint to win the 1989 World Championships. If you ever see a photograph of this event, you'll note not only the elation on Greg Lemond's face but also his prominent biceps muscles. As previously mentioned, squeezing the maximal performance out of your bicycle requires your entire body to contribute. The pull on the handlebars can be immense, and the preacher curl will help hone your biceps strength. For this exercise, try to position your grip width similar to your handlebar position. Imagine yourself sprinting for the line as you slowly bring the weight to your shoulders. With each repetition, feel yourself closing in on the final victory. Remember that form is everything. Don't lift your butt or torque your back to try to complete a repetition. Even when you're fatigued on your bicycle, you want to be smooth and fluid with your motion. The same applies to lifting in the gym. Maintain good control and form throughout the exercise.

⚠️ **SAFETY TIP** Always keep a slight bend at the elbows during the extension phase of the exercise. Overextension can cause ligament strain and injury.

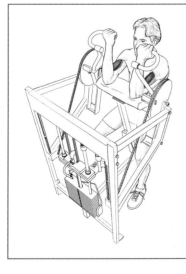

VARIATION

Machine Preacher Curl

Exercise machines are helpful if you are feeling uncomfortable managing the free weights. Grasp the grips of the machine, and place the back of your arms firmly on the pad. Adjust the seat height so your arms rest easily on the pads and your back isn't hunched over. Flex your elbows and bring the grip to your shoulders. Return to the starting position. Some of these machines also give you the option of doing one arm at a time.

Triceps Push-Down

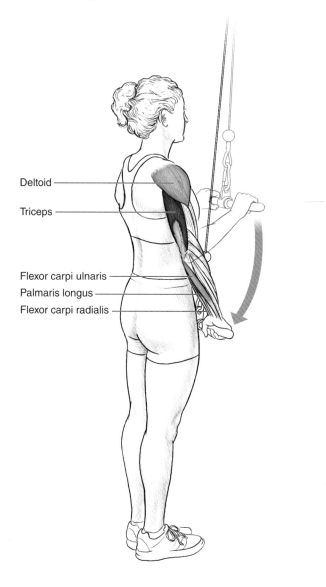

Execution

1. Stand facing a high pulley, and hold the straight-bar attachment using an overhand grip. Your hands should be shoulder-width apart on the bar.
2. Start with the bar at your chest and slowly extend your elbows so your hands travel down to the front of your upper thighs.
3. Keeping your elbows tight to your sides, slowly return to the starting position.

Muscles Involved

Primary: Triceps

Secondary: Deltoid, forearm flexors

Cycling Focus

One of the most common riding positions on a road bike is holding the flat top section (or tops) of the handlebars. This should become a very comfortable position as you train for longer durations. However, when you are riding in this position, your triceps are constantly under stress from your body leaning forward on the handlebars. Therefore, every cyclist needs to have well-conditioned triceps. The triceps push-down simulates this basic "hands on handlebar tops" position on the bike and will prepare you for the training rides that lie ahead. During the exercise, try to position your hands just as you would on your handlebars. A few solid sets of this

exercise in the gym will help eliminate arm fatigue during your rides. Remember that the entire muscle system must be in balance and must support your riding position. If you have weak triceps, your shoulders and lower back will have to overcompensate, resulting in fatigue and discomfort.

VARIATION

Rope Push-Down

Instead of using a straight bar, try this exercise with the rope attachment. As you extend your elbows and pull down on the rope, the exercise will emphasize pronation of your wrists. This will also add the extra dimension of targeting the lateral (outer) head of the triceps. You should perform the exercise just as you would with the bar (as previously described). But at the end of extension, when your arms are nearly straight, you should slightly pull the ends of the rope laterally to both sides (flatten the angle of the rope).

Dumbbell Kickback

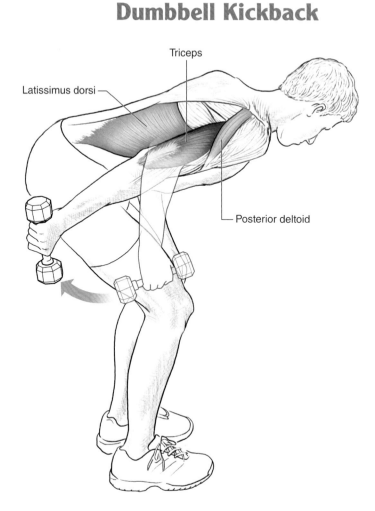

Triceps

Latissimus dorsi

Posterior deltoid

Execution

1. Hold the dumbbell in one hand. Bend at your waist, resting your opposite forearm just above the knee on the same side.
2. Keep your upper arm tight against your body. Your elbow should be bent at 90 degrees, and your lower arm should be pointing toward the floor.
3. Extend your elbow to 180 degrees (arm straight), sweeping the dumbbell backward and upward.

Muscles Involved

Primary: Triceps

Secondary: Latissimus dorsi, posterior deltoid, erector spinae

Cycling Focus

This exercise is ideal because it closely simulates your position on the bike. The dumbbell kickback will help strengthen your arm (primarily your triceps muscle), and it will also help strengthen your back and anterior torso stabilizers. If you simulate the form shown in the illustration, your neck will also be strengthened. Whether you are riding on the flats, climbing, or standing up, your triceps muscles bear a significant portion of your weight. By training in this position, you'll strengthen this key muscle that helps you maintain posture on the bike.

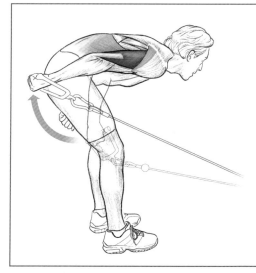

VARIATION

Cable Kickback

You can perform this same exercise using a low cable-pulley system. The benefit of this variation is the constant resistance of the cable when compared to the dumbbell. On the other hand, the advantage of the dumbbell is the increased freedom of movement (thus working your stabilizers) and the added strain on your back and torso.

Bent-Over Cable Triceps Extension

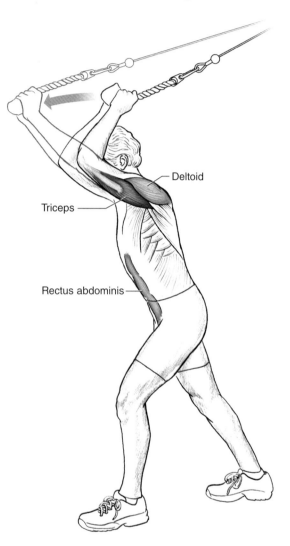

Deltoid

Triceps

Rectus abdominis

Execution

1. Using the rope attachment on a high pulley, face away from the pulley machine and grab the rope above your head. Your elbows should be bent, and your hands should be behind your head.

2. Bend forward at the waist to 45 degrees. Place one foot forward and one foot back for stability.

3. Keeping your upper arms motionless, extend your elbows, pulling the rope forward until your arms are straight and parallel with the ground.

4. Return to the starting position. Switch the front and back foot with each set.

Muscles Involved

Primary: Triceps

Secondary: Deltoid, rectus abdominis

Cycling Focus

As previously mentioned, most of the cycling positions rely on active firing of your triceps muscles. The three riders shown on pages 19 and 21 and this page each have a slightly different (and common) position on the bike, and all of them are relying on their triceps for support. The bent-over triceps extension will help prepare you for all your training miles ahead. When you have proper form on your bike, there is a slight bend in your elbows. Being able to maintain this bend against the weight of your body will require well-developed triceps muscles. In addition, every time you turn the pedals, your bike slightly rocks from side to side. The arms and triceps counter and stabilize this movement. Limiting the lateral movement of your bike provides more available power for forward motion. Another benefit of this exercise is that it will allow you to easily hoist the trophy over your head when all your training has paid off!

VARIATION

Lying Triceps Extension

Lying with your back flat on the bench, extend your elbows, holding the bar above your chest. You should have a fairly narrow grip with your hands slightly closer than shoulder-width apart. Keeping your upper arms (humerus) vertical, bend at the elbows and bring the bar down just above your forehead. Slowly extend your elbows and return to the starting position.

Reverse Barbell Curl

Biceps
Brachialis
Brachioradialis

Extensor carpi radialis longus
Extensor carpi ulnaris
Extensor digitorum

Finish position.

Execution

1. Hold the barbell with your hands shoulder-width apart, palms down. With your elbows extended, rest the barbell against the front of your legs.
2. Keeping your elbows tight to your sides, lift the barbell upward to your shoulders by flexing your elbows.
3. Lower the bar back down to the starting position (elbows extended).
4. For added forearm work, you can bend your wrists back during every repetition of lifting the bar.

Muscles Involved

Primary: Forearm extensors, brachioradialis

Secondary: Biceps, brachialis

Cycling Focus

Cyclists are often amazed at how tired their arms are after a tough descent. Long, technical downhills can test the limits of forearm and grip strength. The reverse barbell curl will strengthen your grip and improve your control of the handlebars. By holding the bar in a palm-down grip during this exercise, you mimic your riding position. Bunny hopping some debris in the road or pulling the front wheel over a dodgy section of road requires you to use the very muscles that this exercise trains. When doing this exercise in the gym, imagine yourself flinging your bike in the air to avoid some lurking hazard.

VARIATIONS

Reverse Barbell Curl on Stability Disks

Standing on stability disks during this exercise will place extra emphasis on your core, back, and lower extremity muscles. You can add stability disks to many of the workouts in this book to increase the degree of difficulty.

Reverse Dumbbell Curl

You can also perform this exercise using dumbbells instead of a barbell. This will further isolate your muscles to ensure that you do not favor one side over the other.

Wrist Extension

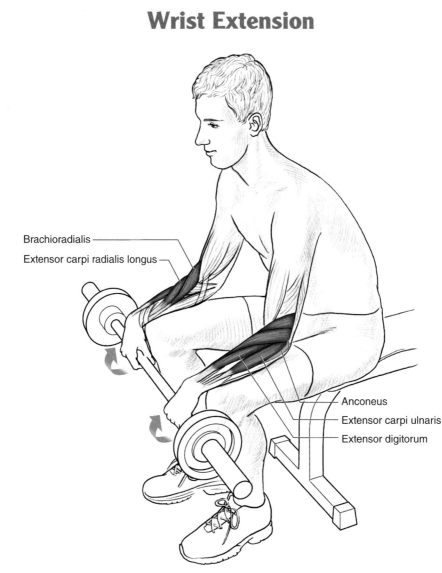

Brachioradialis

Extensor carpi radialis longus

Anconeus

Extensor carpi ulnaris

Extensor digitorum

Execution

1. Sit on a bench and hold the barbell in a palm-down grip. Rest your forearms on your thighs.
2. Bend your wrists toward the floor and lower the barbell.
3. Passing the neutral starting position, extend your wrists toward the ceiling and raise the barbell as high as possible (keep your forearms against your thighs).
4. Return to the lowest barbell position.

Muscles Involved

Primary: Forearm extensors

Secondary: Grip strength

Cycling Focus

Grip strength is extremely important for your safety and bike handling. You never know when you're going to encounter a rough stretch of road. Most cyclists have experienced some scary moments such as hitting a sudden pothole or unpaved patch of road and nearly losing their grip on the handlebars. Imagine riding in the famous Paris-Roubaix, and think about the pain and fatigue the riders must experience in their forearms. Most of us will never have to endure such extreme conditions, but training your grip and forearm strength will improve your bike handling and limit the possibility of losing your grasp on the handlebars.

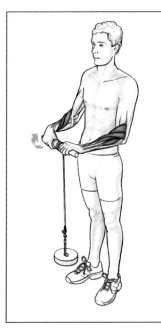

VARIATION

Wrist Roller Palms Down (Spindle Wind)

Many gyms have a small round stick with a rope or chain attached in the middle. Fasten a small weight plate to the far end of the rope. Outstretch your arms and hold the stick in both hands using a palm-down grip. Wind the rope up onto the spindle, raising the weight off the floor. This will work your forearm extensors and also give your deltoids a good workout.

Wrist Curl

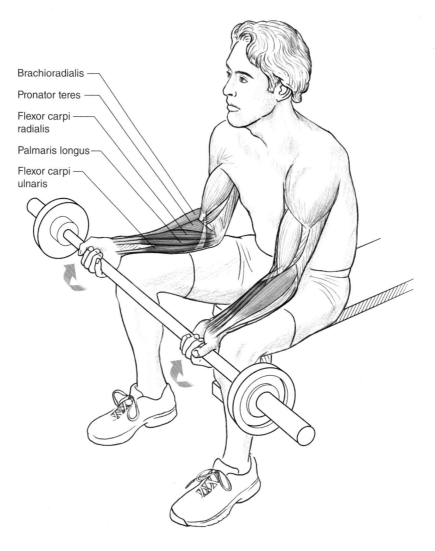

Brachioradialis

Pronator teres

Flexor carpi radialis

Palmaris longus

Flexor carpi ulnaris

Execution

1. Sit on a bench and hold the barbell in a palm-up grip. Rest the back of your forearms on your thighs.
2. Extend your wrists toward the floor and lower the barbell.
3. Passing the neutral starting position, flex your wrists toward the ceiling and raise the barbell as high as possible (keep the back of your forearms against your thighs).

Muscles Involved

Primary: Forearm flexors

Secondary: Grip strength

Cycling Focus

During a sprint, you should be holding the handlebar drops and standing out of the saddle. With each drive of the pedal, you'll aggressively pull back on your hands to counter the torque produced by your leg. Your body weight will also be leaning forward to drive the bike toward the finish line. The sprinting action will strain your entire body, and your forearms are no exception. The wrist curl will specifically target these muscles, increasing your grip strength and forearm strength.

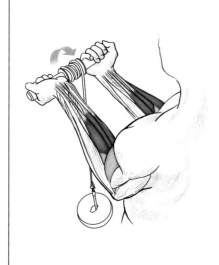

VARIATION

Wrist Roller Palms Up (Spindle Wind)

The wrist roller exercise described in the previous section can also be used to strengthen your forearm flexors. Rather than holding the spindle with your palms down, hold it with your palms up. Keep your arms slightly bent at the elbows. This will also work your biceps muscle. Wind the rope up on the spindle; then lower the weight back to the ground by unwinding the spindle.

The shoulders are continuously strained while you ride. As the primary link between your upper extremities and torso, the shoulder constantly supports the weight of your upper body. Regardless of your position on the bike—standing, sitting, or sprinting—your shoulders fight the force of gravity. At other times, such as during a steep climb or sprint, you'll be pulling hard on the handlebars. This chapter will help you train for all these stressors.

Your deltoid is the primary muscle involved in the powerful movements of the shoulder, and each exercise will focus on a different functional section. This chapter also gives you specific exercises to work your rotator cuff. *Rotator cuff* seems to be a popular term among athletes, and this chapter will help you better understand this group of muscles. The primary role of the rotator cuff is stabilization of the shoulder joint. Many athletes fail to spend time specifically conditioning this important set of muscles. Since the rotator cuff is not as visible as the deltoid, this group of muscles is often forgotten while training in the gym. This is a mistake that can lead to serious shoulder pain and injury.

Your neck also has a tough task when you're on the bike. Whether you're riding on the hoods, tops, or drops of your handlebars, your neck will spend the majority of your ride in an extended position. This will strain the splenius and other neck extensor muscles. In this chapter, you'll find multiple exercises to address this cycling stressor. As previously mentioned, you should train to maintain proper symmetry and balance. To help protect your spinal alignment, this chapter also provides exercises for training the primary neck flexor—the sternocleidomastoid.

I've worked with numerous athletes who have developed neck problems. The causes can be multifactorial, but the two most common culprits are overtraining and poor position on the bike. You should take your time advancing your training program. When you're ramping up your riding volume, include plenty of recovery days to give your body time to adjust. Neck pain and neck problems can be completely debilitating, and working to avoid injury is your best option. By spending time in the gym strengthening your neck, you'll be better prepared for the ongoing strain placed on your neck during training.

Since your shoulders and neck are taxed during your entire ride, proper position is of the utmost importance. If you are too far forward or your handlebars are too low, you may develop early fatigue and face possible injury. There is always a tradeoff between comfort and performance (or aerodynamics) when determining your best fit. Spend time fine-tuning your position before you start training. If you are concerned about your fit, visit your local bicycle retailer or bike club to find a bike fitter. Paying for a professional bike fit is often money well spent.

Even if you train properly and your form is perfect, the very nature of the cycling position will eventually start to strain your neck and shoulders. The bent-forward, head-up position will gradually lead to imbalances in your neck and shoulder musculature. After years of riding, your cervical curve will accentuate, and the intervertebral spaces will narrow posteriorly. Because your arms are extended to the bars and your thoracic spine is bent forward, your scapulae will rotate forward and downward. This will start to strain the muscles stabilizing your shoulder joint. You must work to counter these changes as you train and progress in your cycling career. This chapter will help you train not only your primary cycling muscles, but also the counterbalancing muscles that will help prevent these detrimental changes.

Shoulder Joint

The shoulder is a complicated ball-and-socket joint formed by the proximal end of the humerus and the scapula. Similar to the other ball-and-socket joint—the hip—the structure of the shoulder allows a large degree of mobility. The shoulder allows six primary movements:

Flexion: Elevating your arm in front of you toward your head

Extension: Elevating your arm behind you toward your head

Adduction: Moving your arm inward toward the side of your body

Abduction: Moving your arm outward, away from the side of your body

Internal rotation: Turning your arm and palm downward

External rotation: Turning your arm and palm upward

With high mobility also comes greater potential for injury. The more freedom of movement allowed at a joint, the less fixed support holding the joint in place. This highlights the importance of having a strong and well-conditioned shoulder joint.

Deltoid

As previously discussed, the muscular structure of your shoulder provides a wide range of movement. As a key player in your shoulder movement, the deltoid is a highly developed muscle. The three heads of the deltoid (anterior, lateral, and posterior) combine into a single tendon that inserts onto the humerus (see figure 3.1). The anterior deltoid originates on the clavicle and primarily performs shoulder flexion. The lateral (middle section) deltoid attaches to the acromion and abducts the arm. The posterior (rear) deltoid originates on the scapula and provides shoulder extension. Although there is crossover, this chapter provides specific exercises that focus on each of the three sections of the deltoid.

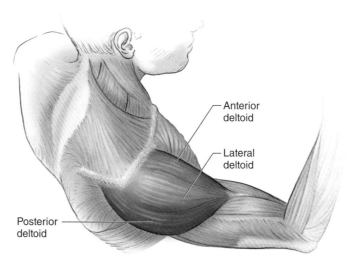

Figure 3.1   Deltoid muscle.

Rotator Cuff

The rotator cuff is a group of shoulder muscles that form a stabilizing and protective shell around the shoulder joint (see figure 3.2). Although they are small in size, these muscles are vital to proper shoulder function. The rotator cuff is composed of four muscles that all attach to various areas of the scapula. The subscapularis is located in the front of the scapula, and the primary role of this muscle is to rotate the arm inward. Behind the scapula lies the infraspinatus muscle and the teres minor. Both of these muscles rotate the arm outward. Finally, the supraspinatus lies on the superior aspect of the scapula. This muscle abducts the shoulder (lifts the arm away from the body) and also rotates the shoulder outward.

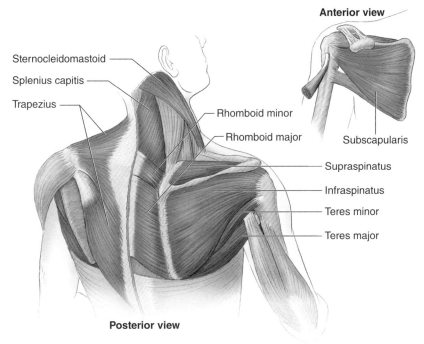

Anterior view

Sternocleidomastoid

Splenius capitis

Trapezius

Rhomboid minor

Rhomboid major

Subscapularis

Supraspinatus

Infraspinatus

Teres minor

Teres major

Posterior view

Figure 3.2   Muscles of the rotator cuff and neck.

Neck Musculature

The neck is a highly mobile and fairly fragile section of the spine. Numerous muscles and ligaments work together to provide this high degree of movement while simultaneously providing adequate stabilization. In this book, we'll focus on the primary movement muscles. The splenius extends the neck (see figure 3.2). It runs along the upper spine and connects to the base of the skull. The trapezius (covered in chapter 5), the levator scapula, and the posterior portion of the sternocleidomastoid all cooperate to aid the splenius in neck extension. Adequate training of all these muscles is vital to your riding health.

The sternocleidomastoid performs front and lateral flexion of the neck and is divided into the sternal head and the clavicular head. As indicated by its name, this muscle connects to the sternum, clavicle, and mastoid of the skull. Long hours on the bike can overemphasize the splenius, and you may find yourself with an underdeveloped sternocleidomastoid. This can potentially cause undue strain on your cervical spine, resulting in pain and disc injury.

Warm-Up and Stretching

Spend 10 minutes warming up the muscles of your neck and shoulders. Jumping rope and rowing on a machine are excellent cardio warm-ups for the exercises in this chapter. After you have the blood moving and the pores open, you should take time to adequately stretch. Your neck and shoulders can be easily injured if you jump into the exercises without a proper warm-up. Shoulder rotations forward and backward, as well as individual stretches, will ensure that your entire joint is loose. The shoulder can rotate through 360 degrees, so make sure you move through your entire range of motion. After stretching the neck forward, backward, and side to side, you can perform some simple isometric exercises to ensure that the neck muscles are ready for your workout. Simply hold your hand against your head to offer resistance to movement. For 10 to 15 seconds, work each group of muscles against the resistance.

Dumbbell Shoulder Press

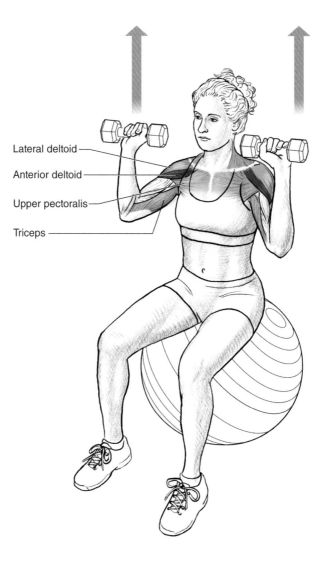

Lateral deltoid
Anterior deltoid
Upper pectoralis
Triceps

Execution

1. Sit on a stability ball and hold the dumbbells with your arms bent and your hands at shoulder level. Your palms should be facing forward.
2. Raise the dumbbells vertically together until your elbows are straight.
3. Lower the dumbbells together back to the starting position.

Muscles Involved

Primary: Anterior deltoid

Secondary: Lateral deltoid, triceps, upper pectoralis, trapezius

Cycling Focus

As mentioned in the introduction to this chapter, the shoulder is constantly under pressure while you are on your bike. Every cycling position relies on the shoulder to counter the weight of the torso as it leans forward on the handlebars. The shoulder press is fundamental to strengthening both your anterior and lateral deltoid. These muscles are key in stabilizing your torso as you pedal. Many cyclists sway from side to side as they ride. Remember that any movement of the bicycle that does not contribute to the forward motion is wasted and should be minimized. Rocking the bike from side to side dissipates energy that could have contributed to the propulsion of your bike.

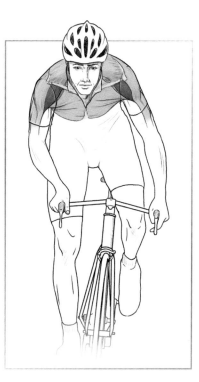

⚠ **SAFETY TIP** Be careful that the ball doesn't roll backward when you are performing this exercise. While keeping your back straight, make sure that your weight and buttocks are slightly forward on the stability ball.

VARIATIONS

Machine Shoulder Press

The machine offers added safety and stability. If you feel nervous about doing the shoulder press with dumbbells or a barbell, the machine is an excellent option.

Barbell Shoulder Press

You can do the same exercise using a barbell. This variation has two options for starting positions. With your hands shoulder-width apart, place the bar across your upper chest or behind your head on your upper back. Raise the barbell above your head until your elbows are straight. Return to the starting position and repeat.

Upright Row

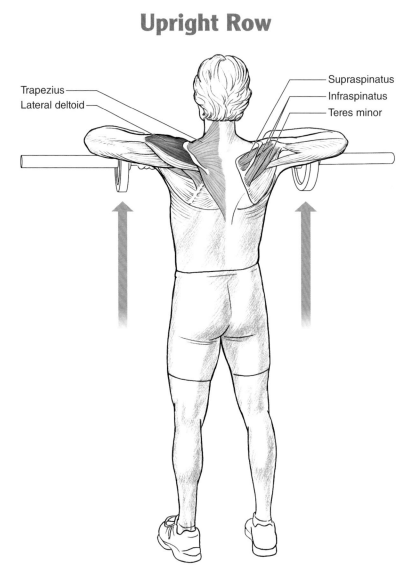

Trapezius
Lateral deltoid

Supraspinatus
Infraspinatus
Teres minor

Execution

1. Hold the barbell with your arms extended down. Use a palm-down grip with your hands positioned slightly narrower than shoulder-width apart.
2. Pull your hands vertically upward to your upper chest, keeping your elbows high.
3. Slowly return to the starting position.

Muscles Involved

Primary: Anterior deltoid, lateral deltoid

Secondary: Infraspinatus, supraspinatus, teres minor, trapezius

Cycling Focus

During a longer climb, you'll likely find your hands resting on the top of the handlebars. If you decide to really hammer your way up the mountain, you'll pull upward on the bar with each turn of the cranks. Watch any climber during a mountainous stage of the Tour de France and you'll see that this is the position the rider assumes once he gets into his climbing rhythm. You should focus on this position while you perform the upright row. This exercise prepares you for your future climbing efforts by strengthening the deltoid, arm, and grip. If you stand and climb with your hands on the hoods—as many riders do when they decide to surge—you'll rely on the muscles trained in this exercise.

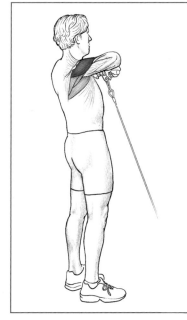

VARIATIONS

Cable Upright Row

You can also use a pulley machine to effectively perform the upright row. Use a straight-handle attachment on a low pulley. Keeping your back straight and your elbows high, pull your hands vertically to your upper chest.

Upright Row on Stability Disks

This is an excellent exercise for using the stability disks. Using stability disks will not only force your lower legs to stabilize your position, but will also train your lower back and torso.

Dumbbell Raise and Sweep

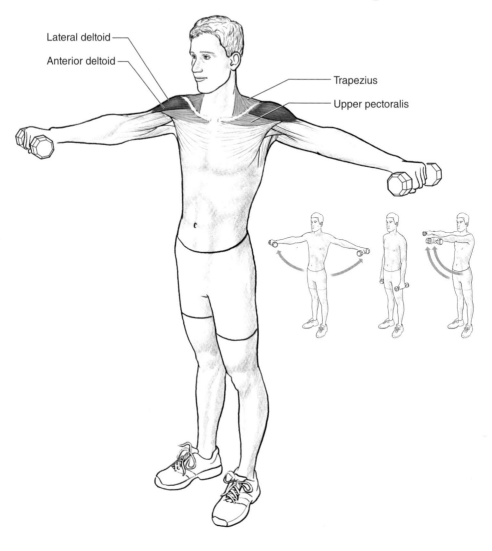

Lateral deltoid

Anterior deltoid

Trapezius

Upper pectoralis

Execution

1. Hold a dumbbell in each hand using a palm-down grip. Your elbows should be extended, and your arms should be at your sides.

2. Keeping both your arms straight at the elbows, lift your right arm upward in front of you until it is parallel with the floor. Simultaneously, lift your left arm upward to the side until it is also parallel with the floor.

3. In the horizontal plane, swap your arm positions. Move your right arm out laterally to your side, and move your left arm straight out in front of you.

4. Lower the dumbbells back to your sides. Repeat the exercise again, alternating the starting position.

Muscles Involved

Primary: Lateral deltoid, anterior deltoid

Secondary: Trapezius, upper pectoralis, posterior deltoid, supraspinatus, erector spinae, torso

Cycling Focus

This is a great exercise for cyclists. It simultaneously works multiple aspects of the shoulder and the core. When you are climbing out of the saddle, you're constantly shifting your weight from side to side to deliver the most power to the pedals. (A similar movement is used when attacking on the flats or sprinting for a finish.) This shifting repeatedly torques your upper body and stresses your shoulder joints. By simulating this movement with both lateral and anterior stressors concurrently, the dumbbell raise and sweep forces your back and torso to fight to keep your upper body from moving. During this exercise, your center of gravity is dynamically shifted, and you have to compensate. Not only will your deltoids get a great workout, but you'll also be adding to your core stability training.

VARIATION

Dumbbell raise and sweep on stability disks: Consider using stability disks to really torture yourself during this exercise.

A-Frame

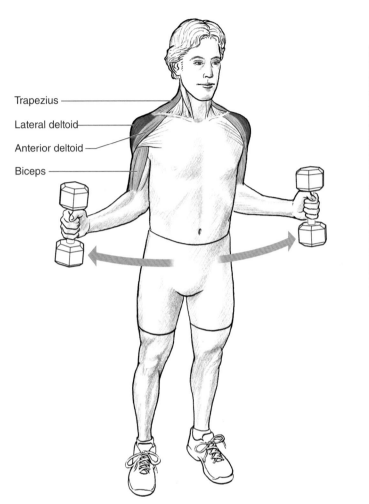

Finish position.

Trapezius
Lateral deltoid
Anterior deltoid
Biceps

Execution

1. Hold the dumbbells with your thumbs up, your elbows at your waist, and your forearms in front of you.
2. Sweep each dumbbell laterally while keeping your forearms parallel with the floor.
3. Keeping your elbows locked at 90 degrees, lift the dumbbells up above your head until they touch.
4. Lower the dumbbells back to the lateral position and then sweep them forward, reversing the motion you previously performed.

Muscles Involved

Primary: Lateral deltoid, subscapularis, infraspinatus, supraspinatus, teres minor

Secondary: Anterior deltoid, posterior deltoid, trapezius, biceps

Cycling Focus

The rotational movement of this exercise specifically targets the rotator cuff. Although cyclists don't often think about training their rotator cuff, its muscles are vitally important for almost every athlete. When you're in your riding position, the rotator cuff locks the shoulder into place, giving you a platform on which to support your body weight. This is fundamental to a stable shoulder, and if you have a weak

or underdeveloped rotator cuff, the constant forces that riding places on your shoulder will cause pain and discomfort. Cyclists who have sustained a rotator cuff injury during a crash can attest to how much discomfort they have when trying to rehabilitate on their bicycle.

Dumbbell external rotation.

Dumbbell internal rotation.

VARIATIONS

Dumbbell External Rotation

Lie with your back and elbow resting on a bench. Holding a dumbbell, lay your forearm across your waist so it is parallel to the floor. Keeping your upper arm in tight to your body, rotate your shoulder so that your forearm moves in an arching motion from your waist to a vertical position. Return to the starting position.

Dumbbell Internal Rotation

Lie with your back and elbow resting on a bench. Holding a dumbbell, lay your forearm out to the side so it is parallel with the floor or the bench. Keeping your upper arm in tight to your body, rotate your shoulder so that your forearm moves in an arching motion from the bench to a vertical position.

Note: You can combine the external and internal rotation exercise and complete an entire 180-degree sweep with your arm.

Stability Ball Dumbbell Raise

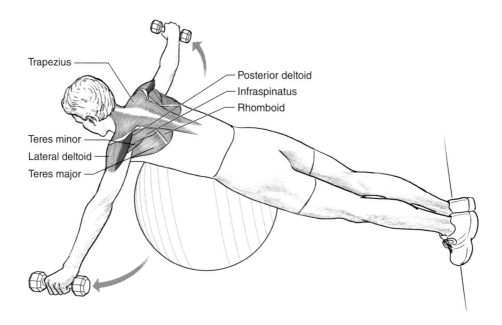

Trapezius

Posterior deltoid

Infraspinatus

Rhomboid

Teres minor

Lateral deltoid

Teres major

Execution

1. Place your feet against a wall and rest the front of your hips and abdomen on a large stability ball.
2. Hold a dumbbell in each hand and let your arms hang vertically downward toward the floor. Your thumbs should be facing upward.
3. Keeping your elbows straight, raise your hands in an arching motion until they are at 90 degrees to each side and parallel with the floor.
4. Return to the starting position.

Muscles Involved

Primary: Posterior deltoid

Secondary: Lateral deltoid, trapezius, rhomboid, infraspinatus, teres minor, teres major, erector spinae

Cycling Focus

Essentially, two forces are placed on your arms and shoulders while you are riding. The first is the constant downward force placed on the bars by your body weight and body position. The second is the upward pull of your arms on the bars when you are sprinting or climbing. The bent-over dumbbell raise focuses on the muscles used in the latter and develops the posterior aspect of your shoulder. Because most of your time on the bike is spent leaning forward, much of the shoulder development that occurs while riding will be to your anterior shoulder. That is why this gym exercise is so important. Remember that your body is designed for symmetry. To balance the anterior

muscle development, you will need to focus on this exercise to train your posterior shoulder. This will help properly align your shoulder joint and prevent aggravating injuries.

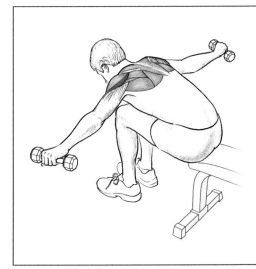

Bent-Over Dumbbell Raise on Bench

If you feel unstable on the stability ball or it puts too much strain on your back, you can perform this same exercise sitting on a bench. Bend over so your chest is nearly resting on your knees. Keep your elbows straight and your arms down at your sides. Slowly raise your arms out to each side until they are parallel with the floor.

Single-Arm Dumbbell Row

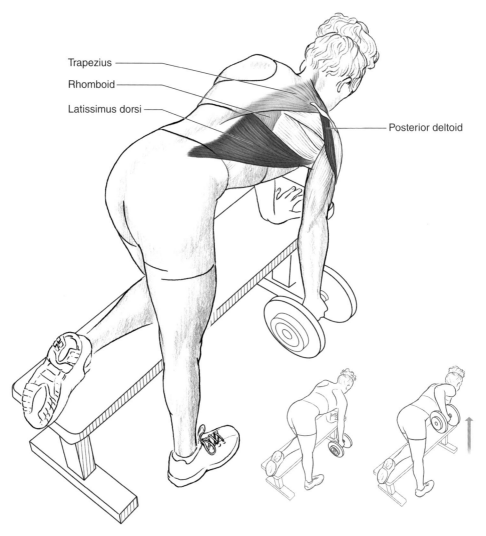

Trapezius

Rhomboid

Latissimus dorsi

Posterior deltoid

Execution

1. Rest your knee and same-side hand on the bench. Keep your back parallel with the floor.
2. Hold a dumbbell in your opposite hand and let your arm hang vertically toward the floor.
3. Bring your hand upward until your hand reaches your chest. Your elbow should brush against your side as your arm moves upward.
4. Return to the starting position.

Muscles Involved

Primary: Posterior deltoid, latissimus dorsi

Secondary: Trapezius, rhomboid, biceps

Cycling Focus

In the illustration of this exercise, you can see its similarity to the cycling position. While doing this exercise in the gym, you should think about sprinting powerfully on your bike. When you stand up to sprint, you'll not only be crashing down on the pedals, but you'll also perform huge pulls on the bars with your arms. The single-arm dumbbell row will simulate this surging pull of your arms and help you get every ounce of energy out of your sprint. When doing the exercise, imagine yourself in a sprint finish, fighting for the victory. Try to feel each arm pulling on the handlebar as your muscles scream under the strain.

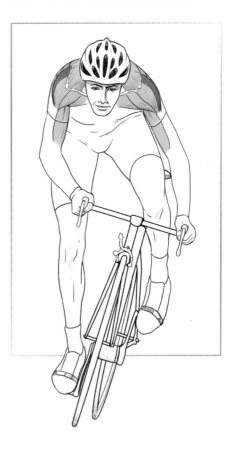

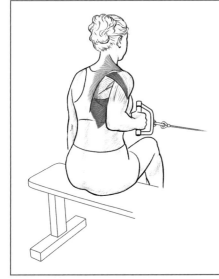

VARIATION

Single-Arm Cable Pull

Sitting on a bench or stability ball, hold the handle for the low pulley with one hand. Place your other hand on your knee for stability. Let your arm fully extend in front of you. Pull your hand back to your side, keeping your elbow and arm tight to your body.

Floor Bridge

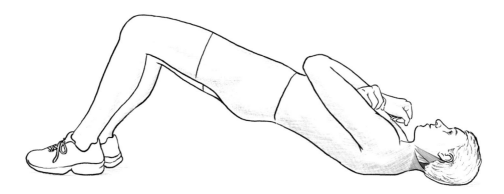

Execution

1. Lie on the floor on your back. Pull your feet up toward your buttocks, and cross your arms on your chest.
2. By looking upward and behind you, slowly extend your neck back, lifting your shoulders and body off the floor. Keep your back straight.
3. Slowly roll your neck forward, returning to the starting position.

Muscles Involved

Primary: Splenius capitis

Secondary: Trapezius, levator scapula, erector spinae, posterior sternocleidomastoid

Sternocleidomastoid

Splenius capitis

Trapezius

Levator scapula

Cycling Focus

This is a fundamental exercise for a healthy neck, especially when you spend a lot of time on your bike. The majority of your riding time will be spent with your neck in extension. If you take time off from the bike and then start riding again, you may often find that your neck is the sorest part of your body. A strong neck will help maintain proper spinal alignment and help prevent problems in the future. When you initially perform this exercise, you must be sure not to overdo it. You may feel great while in the gym, but soreness will often creep up on you the next day. A few years back in the Race Across America, a competitor's neck became so fatigued from the constant extension that he couldn't even look up. His mechanic had to do some improvisation. He devised a support splint connected to the rider's shoulders and helmet that held his head upright so he could see where he was going!

⚠ **SAFETY TIP** Make sure you are well stretched before doing this exercise. You must also ensure that you don't overextend your neck. Avoid arching your neck so that the weight is resting on the top of your head.

Neck Extender

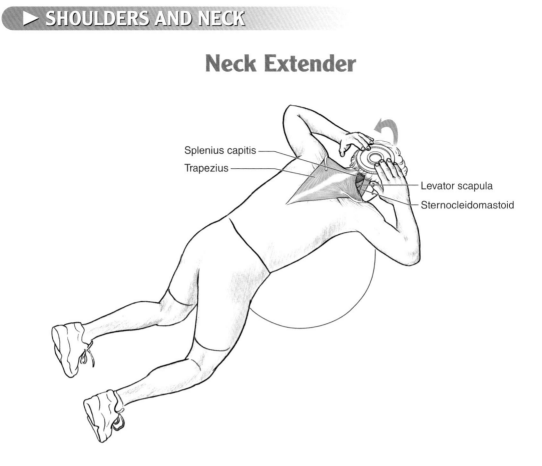

Splenius capitis

Trapezius

Levator scapula

Sternocleidomastoid

Execution

1. Kneel beside a stability ball. Lean your chest on the ball and hold a weight plate on the back of your head.
2. Start with your neck flexed forward. Slowly extend your neck and raise your head until you are mimicking the neck position you use while riding.
3. Return to the starting position.

Muscles Involved

Primary: Splenius capitis

Secondary: Trapezius, levator scapula, erector spinae, posterior sternocleidomastoid

Cycling Focus

Because the neck extenders are so challenged while you are riding, I've included two exercises that focus on these muscles specifically. Think about the extreme neck extension needed when in an aerodynamic time-trialing position. Although you may never need to time trial, almost every riding position forces your neck to hold your head up so you can see the road. This exercise is excellent at mimicking this position and really focuses on the muscles used while riding. With all the neck exercises, you must remember to start with lower weights and work your way up. The point of the exercise is to help you avoid injury on your bike, so don't hurt yourself while working out in the gym!

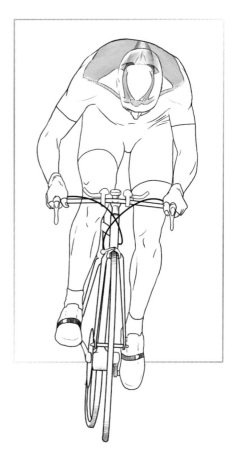

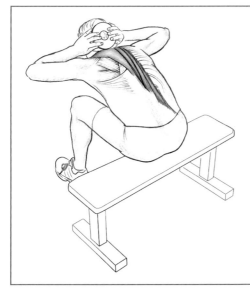

VARIATION

Neck Extender on Bench

If leaning over on the stability ball is difficult on your back or knees, you can perform this same exercise while sitting on a bench. This will offer more stability while still focusing on the same muscles.

Neck Flexor

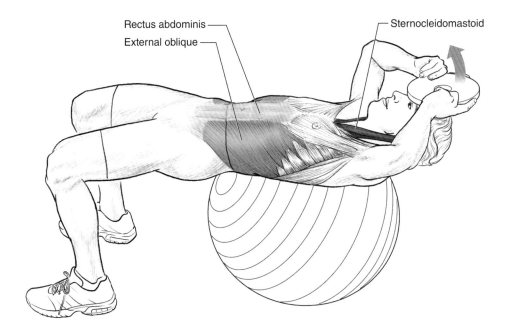

Rectus abdominis
External oblique
Sternocleidomastoid

Execution

1. Lie with your shoulder blades resting on the stability ball. Hold a weight plate with both hands on your forehead.
2. Start with your neck extended (head back). Slowly flex your neck and raise your head upward, chin toward your chest.
3. Return to the starting position.

Muscles Involved

Primary: Sternocleidomastoid

Secondary: Rectus abdominis, external oblique, internal oblique

Cycling Focus

As mentioned, good health and fitness are all about balance. Because cycling places such a strain on your neck extenders, these muscles can become more developed than your sternocleidomastoid. If this occurs, the neck extenders can unduly stress the posterior aspect of your spine and cause asymmetry. Over time, this asymmetry can misalign your spine and cause pain. A well-known cyclist and friend of mine had to completely stop cycling in his 50s because his neck caused him so much pain. After six months of physical therapy—balancing his neck and back muscles—he was back on the bike and riding pain free.

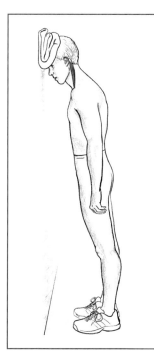

VARIATION

Wall Neck Flexor

A simple variation of the neck flexor exercise can be done almost anywhere. Lean forward and place your forehead against a wall (you may use a pad for comfort). Flex your neck so your eyes look toward the floor. Return to the starting position.

Side Neck Lift

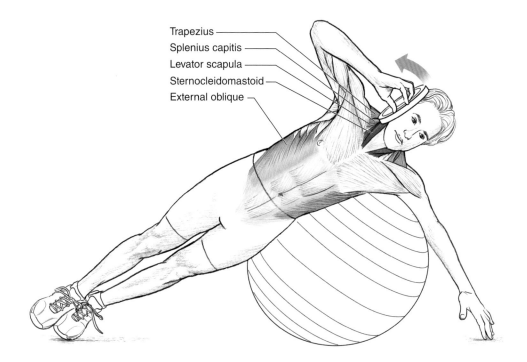

Trapezius
Splenius capitis
Levator scapula
Sternocleidomastoid
External oblique

Execution

1. Lie on your side with one arm draped over the stability ball. Hold a small weight plate with your opposite hand against the side of your head.

2. Start with your downward-facing ear near your shoulder. Keep your eyes looking forward, and laterally flex your neck until your upward ear is nearly touching your shoulder.

3. Return to the starting position. Repeat, switching sides.

Muscles Involved

Primary: Sternocleidomastoid

Secondary: Splenius capitis, erector spinae, levator scapula, trapezius, external oblique, internal oblique

Cycling Focus

The sternocleidomastoid allows you to look back to check your opposition while racing. The primary focus of the side neck lift is to help you develop neck stability. More important, this exercise will help keep your spine properly aligned. The vertebral foramen is the passage in the middle of your vertebrae. Through this space, the spinal cord courses down your spine, protected from injury or damage. Poor spinal alignment can cause one or more of the vertebrae to impinge on this space, which will cause significant pain as well as potential functional deficits.

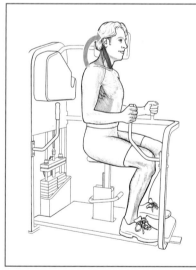

VARIATION

Machine Lateral Neck Flexion

For all the neck exercises, you may choose to use a machine. Lever machines are easy to use, and they provide you with extra stability while performing an exercise.

Most cyclists don't spend much time developing their chest muscles. However, these muscles are important when taking the entire cyclist into consideration. The chest plays a fundamental role in connecting the rider to the bicycle via the shoulders and arms. As previously discussed, symmetry and balance are needed in order to enhance performance and avoid injury. A truly fit rider is one who has strong and balanced musculature; a cyclist needs a solid foundation to optimally perform. Whenever you're riding, your back will be hypertrophying because of the strain of the cycling position. Because the chest muscles are mainly employed during extreme efforts such as climbing or sprinting, these muscles may not undergo the same adaptation as your back during your training rides. Therefore, you'll have to pay special attention to your chest muscles while working out in the gym.

Your work in the gym will also pay off when you surge on your bicycle. Every time a cyclist powers up a climb or sprints away from the field, the chest muscles will be firing with a vengeance. The powerful downstroke of the leg will force the bike to swing to the side. This movement is countered by the stabilization of the bike at the handlebars. Without a solid foundation, much of the power transfer to the bike would be lost. Next time you see the end of a bike race, pay attention to the cyclists' upper bodies and how each cyclist throws his complete self into the sprint. The chest, arms, and legs all help hurl the straining cyclist to the line.

Chest Musculature

The chest muscles are shown in figure 4.1 on page 56. The pectoralis major is the primary muscle of the chest, and it is composed of two anatomical sections that are each shaped like a triangle. The upper section, or clavicular head, connects to the clavicle and the manubrium of the sternum. It inserts onto the upper portion of the humerus. The lower section, or sternal head, of the pectoralis major originates on the sternum. The sternal head inserts just under the upper head of the pectoralis major on the humerus.

The primary role of the pectoralis major is adduction, flexion, and internal rotation of the arm at the shoulder joint. This allows your arm to make strong movements across the chest—such as moving your handlebars from side to side. Although there are only two anatomical sections of the pectoralis major, this muscle can be divided into three fairly distinct functional sections. Different muscle fibers in each of these three functional areas are activated based on the arm's angle with respect to the shoulder joint. The exercises in this chapter are grouped according to this functional delineation, and divided into upper, middle, and lower focus points. During all these exercises, the entire pectoralis major is trained, but various sections will bear the majority of the workload.

The pectoralis minor is a small, externally nonvisible muscle that lies under the pectoralis major. The pectoralis minor originates on the upper margin of the third, fourth, and fifth ribs. All the fibers come together and insert on the coracoid process of the scapula. The primary role of the pectoralis minor is to lower the angle of the scapula, thus pulling the shoulder forward.

The serratus anterior muscle forms the side of your chest. This muscle wraps around the outside of the upper eight ribs and inserts along the length of the medial scapula. Its role is to pull the scapula forward and around the rib cage, similar to the motion that occurs when throwing a punch. That's why this muscle is sometimes referred to as the "boxer's muscle." For the cyclist, the serratus anterior helps stabilize the scapula and shoulder. Many of the exercises in this chapter and chapter 6 will help develop the serratus anterior.

The anterior muscles of the chest are fewer and simpler when compared to the numerous muscles of the back. The three primary chest muscles (pectoralis major, pectoralis minor, and serratus anterior) will bear all the workload and counterbalancing duties. During your workouts, focus on the individual part of the muscle being trained (as described by the workout), and think about how this muscle will enhance your performance on the road.

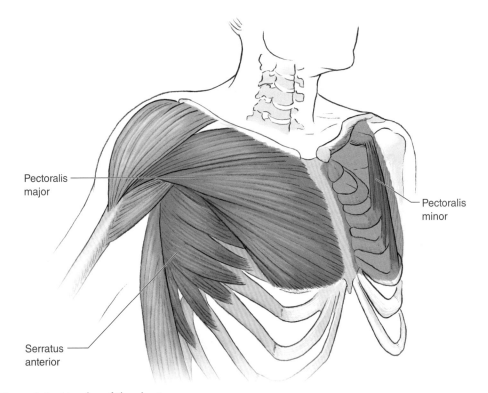

Pectoralis major

Pectoralis minor

Serratus anterior

Figure 4.1   Muscles of the chest.

Warm-Up and Stretching

Warm up for 5 to 10 minutes with some sort of cardio work—treadmill, stair stepper, or rowing machine. Once you develop a sweat, focus on stretching your anterior torso. Stretch your chest by lying on the floor in the push-up position. Allow the pectoralis major and minor to stretch for 15 to 30 seconds. This works even better if push-up handles are available. Slowly perform a few knee-down push-ups until you feel warm. You can also warm up using the dip bars. Standing on a platform, mimic the dip motion. Using your legs as an aid, hold yourself in the down, arms-flexed position of a dip. Repeat this motion very slowly multiple times to adequately stretch your chest and arms.

Dip

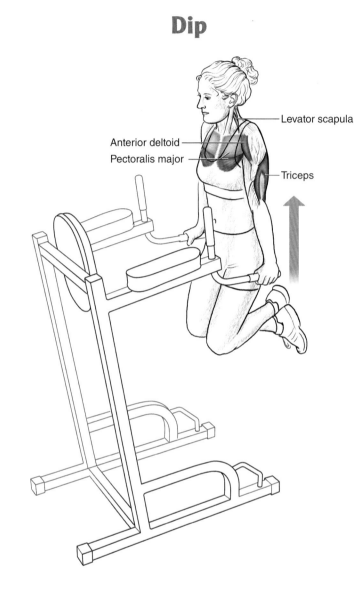

Levator scapula

Anterior deltoid

Pectoralis major

Triceps

Execution

1. Hold the dip bars with your arms extended and your chest leaning forward.
2. Bend your elbows and lower your body until your upper arms are parallel with the floor (elbows are bent to 90 degrees).
3. Push yourself back up to the starting position.

Muscles Involved

Primary: Lower pectoralis major, triceps

Secondary: Anterior deltoid, latissimus dorsi, pectoralis minor, levator scapula, teres major, rhomboid

Cycling Focus

Comparing the exercise illustration with a cyclist sprinting allows you to see the value in this workout. The dip is my favorite chest training exercise because it works so many muscles that support the upper body of the cyclist. The chest plays a key role in stability, power, and steering control when you are sprinting on your bike. The strength of your pectoralis major will allow you to steady the side-to-side movement of your bike while your legs produce a tremendous amount of torque during the sprint. All the energy of your legs should be used for forward propulsion, not frantically swinging the bike from side to side. The dip exercise will also strengthen your entire shoulder joint, providing added support and endurance for the countless hours you'll spend leaning forward on your handlebars.

VARIATION

Machine dip: Dip assist machines can be used if you are unable to perform the exercise without any aid. Generally, these machines include a platform to place your knees on while you hold the dip handles. You dial in a weight setting, and the platform assists you in lifting and lowering your body during the exercise.

Decline Dumbbell Press

Anterior deltoid

Pectoralis major

Triceps

Execution

1. Set the decline bench at a downward angle of 20 to 40 degrees. Lie on the bench and hold a dumbbell in each hand. Your arms should be extended, and your palms should be facing away from your head.

2. Lower the dumbbells together to your chest. Your palms should continue to face away from your head.

3. Push the dumbbells up until you return to the starting position.

Muscles Involved

Primary: Lower pectoralis major

Secondary: Triceps, anterior deltoid

Cycling Focus

The position for the decline dumbbell press mimics your position on the bike when climbing with your hands on the hoods. As you stand out of your saddle to climb, you'll be leaning forward with your torso to help drive the pedals around. This will increase the strain placed on your arms, shoulders, and chest. Your lower pectoralis major will help steady your bike and support the weight of your body over the bars. With each pedal stroke, your bike will want to rock from side to side. Your pectoralis major will keep this movement in check and help keep your form efficient.

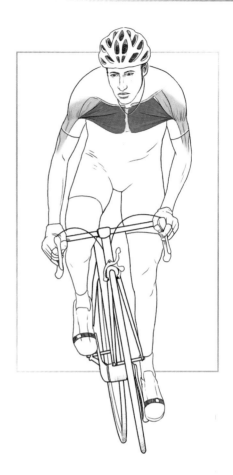

VARIATION

Decline barbell press: The barbell adds extra stability to the decline press exercise. As you lower the bar, it will stop when it hits your chest. This will limit the potential for overflexion injury. The downside of using the bar is that it limits each arm's freedom and range of motion. The more unstable the arms are during the exercise, the more the accessory muscles will need to be conditioned in order for you to maintain proper form.

Cable Crossover

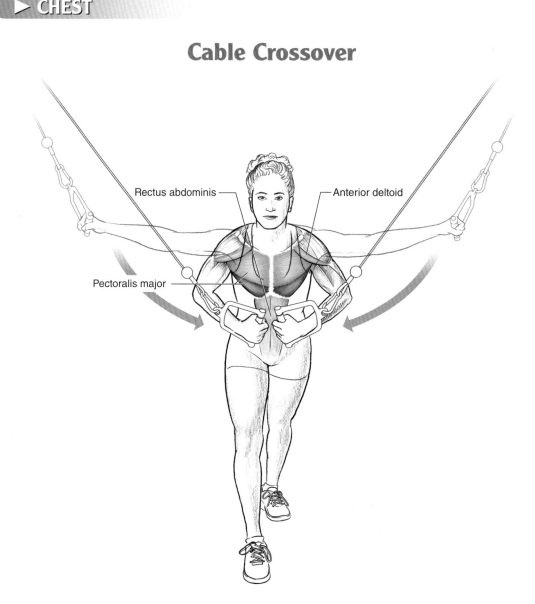

Rectus abdominis

Anterior deltoid

Pectoralis major

Execution

1. Grasp a high pulley handle in each hand and lean slightly forward. Your arms should be out to the sides with only a slight bend in the elbow.
2. Keeping your elbows locked, bring the handles together until your knuckles touch in front of your waist.
3. Slowly return your hands to the starting position.

Muscles Involved

Primary: Lower pectoralis major

Secondary: Anterior deltoid, rectus abdominis, forearm flexors

Cycling Focus

The start of the time trial is one of the more explosive moments in cycling. You need to quickly go from a standstill to race speed. The bike often has aero wheels and aero bars that can add to the inertia of the bike. As the clock clicks down and the referee lets you roll out, you'll be driving the pedals with your entire might. With each leg driving downward, your upper body will be pulling to counteract the extreme force. This will require your pectoralis major, biceps, and abdominal muscles to forcefully contract. The cable crossover will help develop your body's ability to execute this powerful contraction.

VARIATION

Seated Cable Crossover

You can perform this same exercise while seated on a stability ball. This is more difficult and will require additional activation of your abdominal muscles. You'll notice that your entire core will be firm and contracting to keep your position stable.

Bench Press

Anterior deltoid

Triceps

Pectoralis major

Execution

1. Keeping your back flat on the bench, grab the bar with a grip that is slightly wider than shoulder width.
2. Starting with your elbows extended, slowly lower the bar to your chest.
3. Without bouncing the bar off your chest, return the bar to the starting position.

Muscles Involved

Primary: Middle pectoralis major

Secondary: Anterior deltoid, triceps

Cycling Focus

The bench press is one of the best-known exercises in the gym. It primarily works the pectoralis major muscles while allowing support of the back and spine. Cyclists can benefit from this exercise because it mimics the rider's basic position on the bike. Whether your hands are on the tops, hoods, or drops of your handlebars, your pectoralis major will play the primary role in supporting your body. Look at the illustration here and you'll see that the starting position in the bench press is very similar to your position while cruising on your bike. The long miles spent on your bike will slowly fatigue your body, and the better condition all your supporting muscles are in, the better you will ride.

⚠ **SAFETY TIP** Avoid arching your back when lifting the weight. This puts unnecessary strain on your back and prevents isolation of your pectoralis major.

VARIATION

Machine chest press: The machine chest press offers two advantages over the barbell bench press. The weight is easier to set up and adjust, and the machine provides more support. Remember to keep your back flat against the pad during the exercise. Form is more important than lifting a heavier weight.

Dumbbell Bench Press on Stability Ball

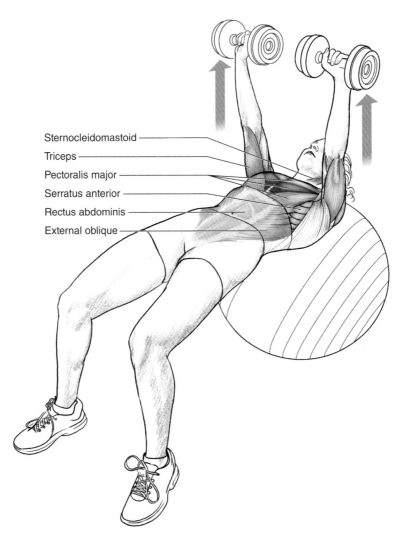

Sternocleidomastoid
Triceps
Pectoralis major
Serratus anterior
Rectus abdominis
External oblique

Execution

1. Lie back with your shoulders on a stability ball, keeping your neck and head off the ball. Hold a dumbbell in each hand with your arms extended above your chest. Your palms should be facing toward your feet.

2. Starting with your arms fully extended, lower the dumbbells together until they are at the level of your chest.

3. Slowly return to the starting position.

Muscles Involved

Primary: Middle pectoralis major

Secondary: Anterior deltoid, triceps, sternocleidomastoid, rectus abdominis, external oblique, internal oblique, serratus anterior

Cycling Focus

I love this exercise because it not only works the arms and chest, but also works the neck flexors and abdominal muscles. The instability of the exercise ball adds an increased degree of difficulty; therefore, you'll likely have to use a lighter weight than you use when performing the barbell bench press. When using a barbell or a machine, your weak arm will often gain extra support from your strong arm during the bench press. By working with dumbbells on an unstable ball, you'll definitely be forcing all your accessory muscles as well as each pectoralis major to perform their fair share of the work. Again, you can see that the exercise position closely resembles a common position on the bike.

VARIATION

Single-arm dumbbell bench press: Mix this variation into one of the sets when performing the dumbbell bench press. By working one arm at a time, you will increase the work of your trunk stabilizers. You will find that this places extra stress on your abdominal muscles, obliques, and back.

Medicine Ball Push-Up

Triceps
Anterior deltoid
Pectoralis major

External oblique
Rectus abdominis
(under aponeurosis)

Execution

1. Assume the standard push-up position, but place one hand on a medicine ball and the other hand on the floor. Keep your back straight and flat.
2. Keeping your back flat with the plane of the ground, lower yourself until your chest nearly touches the ground.
3. Return to the starting position (elbow extended).
4. Repeat the set with the medicine ball on the opposite side.

Muscles Involved

Primary: Middle pectoralis major

Secondary: Anterior deltoid, triceps, rectus abdominis, external oblique, internal oblique, serratus anterior

Cycling Focus

The push-up is an excellent training exercise for cyclists. This exercise doesn't add much bulk, but it strengthens your arms, chest, shoulders, back, and torso. By adding the medicine ball, you'll get increased range and flexibility as well as stronger muscles. During your rides, you'll spend almost all of your time in a position that is similar to the push-up position. A stable body sets a strong foundation to power the pedals. When fatigue sets in, you'll start to lose form. And as your form falters, your efficiency will wane. You can add strength and endurance to your rides by working the push-up in the gym.

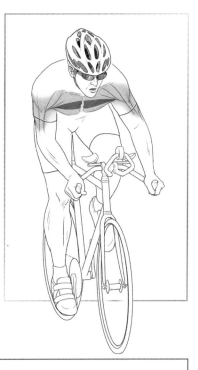

VARIATION

Stability Ball Push-Up

Doing push-ups on the stability ball adds an extra degree of difficulty. Not only do you need to perform the push-up motion, but you also need to stabilize your body to keep the ball from moving. Additionally, you have to compress the sides of the ball inward so that your hands don't slip downward to the floor. Start this exercise with your feet on the floor (see figure a). If you want increased difficulty, try to perform the push-up with your feet resting on top of a bench (see figure b). Once you've mastered the bench version, try lifting one foot off the bench while keeping your knee straight. This makes the exercise very tough.

⚠ SAFETY TIP Make sure you work up to this variation. If you don't have a good grip on the stability ball, your hands can slip, which may result in injury.

Incline Dumbbell Press

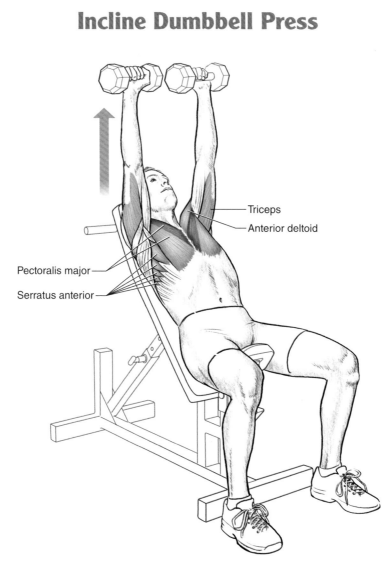

Triceps

Anterior deltoid

Pectoralis major

Serratus anterior

Execution

1. Sit on an incline bench and hold the dumbbells using a palm-out grip. Your arms should be extended.
2. Lower both dumbbells vertically until your elbows are flexed and the dumbbells are at chest level.
3. Slowly return the dumbbells to the starting position.

Muscles Involved

Primary: Upper pectoralis major

Secondary: Anterior deltoid, triceps, serratus anterior

Cycling Focus

You've been on a solo break, and now it comes to this: You're sprinting toward the finish line, and you can sense the other riders closing in and wanting to swallow you up. You make a last surge for the line and throw your bike forward to just nose out the rider next to you. Fortunately, you were ready because you trained so hard. The incline press enabled you to train the very muscles you used to thrust your bike in front of your opponent at the last minute. You'll also achieve other gains from this exercise. Like the other exercises in this chapter, the incline press will fortify your torso stability and help prevent the fatigue that can result from spending the day leaning forward on your handlebars.

VARIATION

Incline barbell press: Another option is using a barbell on an incline bench. This will offer you added stability and limit the downward movement because the bar will rest on your chest. If you find it difficult to set up the exercise with dumbbells and to keep them steady, then the barbell is a good option for you.

Stability Ball Dumbbell Fly

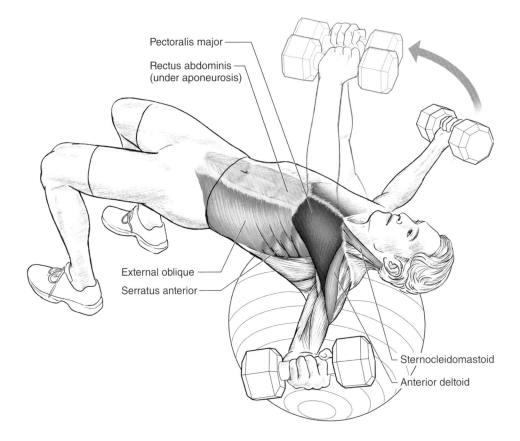

Pectoralis major

Rectus abdominis
(under aponeurosis)

External oblique

Serratus anterior

Sternocleidomastoid

Anterior deltoid

Execution

1. Lie back with your shoulders on a stability ball, keeping your neck and head off the ball. Hold a dumbbell in each hand with your palms facing inward.

2. Start with your arms out to the sides. Your elbows should have a slight bend (150-degree angle between the upper arm and the forearm).

3. Keeping your elbow angle fixed, slowly bring the dumbbells together above your chest.

4. Return to the starting position.

Muscles Involved

Primary: Pectoralis major

Secondary: Anterior deltoid, sternocleidomastoid, rectus abdominis, external oblique, internal oblique, serratus anterior

Cycling Focus

The end of a time trial is brutal. You've given everything you have out on the road, and now you have to motivate your machine to show a burst of speed for the last 100 meters. With each trouncing of a pedal, your bike will want to swing out to the side. Your arms and chest prevent the movement from sapping too much of your power or control. You can see from the image that the cyclist's arm position is close to the position of the dumbbell fly workout. Remember, you want all the energy to be moving your bike forward. Therefore, you need to use your pectoralis major to maintain the vertical plane of the bicycle.

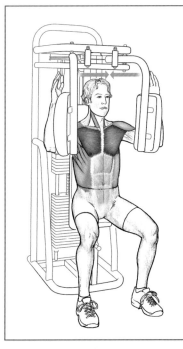

VARIATION

Pec Deck

The pec deck isolates the pectoralis major. Make sure you use good form and keep your back tight against the pad. Focus on using your pecs rather than trying to manipulate your arm position to get extra leverage.

Dumbbell Pullover

Triceps
Posterior deltoid
Teres major
Pectoralis major
Latissimus dorsi
Serratus anterior

Execution

1. While lying with your back on a stability ball, grasp the inside edge of the weight plate of a dumbbell with both hands.
2. Starting with the dumbbell above your chest, and keeping a slight bend in your elbows, slowly lower the dumbbell downward and backward until it reaches the level of your head.
3. Keeping your elbow angle consistent, bring the weight back up to the vertical position by rotating at the shoulders.

Muscles Involved

Primary: Pectoralis major

Secondary: Latissimus dorsi, serratus anterior, teres major, posterior deltoid, triceps, rhomboid, pectoralis minor

Cycling Focus

Powering through a long straightaway on a time-trial bike will force you to use many of the muscles trained in this exercise. Midway through the motion of this exercise, you'll find that the position is very similar to a rider stretched out in aero bars. During each forceful pedal stroke, you'll pull back on the bars to drive your foot through the pedals. Simply put, the key to time trialing is going fast. A professional racer and friend of mine recently had a revelation about riding fast in time trials. He said, "You just have to step on the pedals harder—secret of the pros!"

VARIATION

Machine pullover: Getting into position for this exercise on a stability ball can be awkward and difficult. The pullover machine offers a good alternative and works the same muscles.

The importance of a strong and fit back cannot be overemphasized. Your back and spine provide the foundation for almost every activity that you perform, and cycling is no exception. Unfortunately, back problems are a frequent complaint of cyclists. Because of the bent-over position on a bike, your back muscles are constantly engaged. This stress can wreak havoc on your body if you're not conditioned and trained to withstand the ongoing effort. In addition to withstanding the strain of your position, your back must also provide a solid base that enables you to generate power during your pedal stroke. Your back muscles stabilize your spine and pelvis, allowing your legs to generate maximal power.

The best strategy for a healthy back is to proactively condition yourself to avoid any problems before they arise. The exercises in this chapter will help you do just that. You should start slow and use lighter weights during your early workouts. Take your time building strength in your back—this will pay dividends in the long run. When starting out slow, you may often think that the weight is too light. Be patient. The early work lays the foundation for your future training with heavier weights. Even if you think you are lifting a minimum load, you'll often feel the effects a day or two after the workout. Remember, adaptation occurs during your rest days, so be sure to let your muscles adequately recover. This includes not doing a huge ride the day after you do a back workout in the gym.

This chapter contains exercises that will prepare your back for the stressors of riding and racing. As with many of the exercises in this book, the exercises for your back will involve some crossover, which means multiple muscles will be worked by the same exercise. However, your focus should be on the muscle groups listed under each exercise. This will help you get the most out of your training, and by thinking about specific muscle groups, your form will likely improve both in and out of the gym.

Skeletal Anatomy

The spine is the fundamental pillar of your body. It includes 7 cervical vertebrae (C1-C7), 12 thoracic vertebrae (T1-T12), 5 lumbar vertebrae (L1-L5), a fused sacrum (S1-S5), and a fused coccyx. All support and movement of your torso is made possible by the stacked vertebrae housing the spinal cord. Each vertebra has multiple contact points with the vertebra above and below it (see figure 5.1 on page 78). These contact points are called articular facets. At each level, a lateral canal (intervertebral foramen) is formed that allows nerves to extend from the spinal cord to various destinations throughout the body. A large number of ligaments help stabilize and hold the vertebral bodies together.

Intervertebral discs cushion the intersection between two vertebrae and allow smooth movement of the spine. The fibrous outer section of the disc is called the annulus fibrosus. The inner section, which helps distribute pressure and stress, is called the nucleus pulposus. A herniated disc occurs when there is a breakdown of the fibrous outer band

and a bulging out of the nucleus pulposus. This bulge can happen anywhere around the disc, but when it happens near the vertebral foramen, it can compress the exiting nerve and cause excruciating pain and weakness.

Cyclists have a tendency to develop back problems because the riding position places anatomical stressors on the curved spine. Normally, the lower back has a lordotic curve that causes the lumbar spine to appear to bend inward. When you ride your bike, this curve is flattened. Cyclists like to ride with a "flat back" because it improves aerodynamics. However, the flattening of your lordotic curve can place increased pressure on the anterior aspect of your lumbar vertebrae and intervertebral discs. If the force becomes too great, disc herniation can result. By easing into your training and working the muscles of your back and abdomen in the gym, you can alleviate many of the problems that may arise from your cycling position.

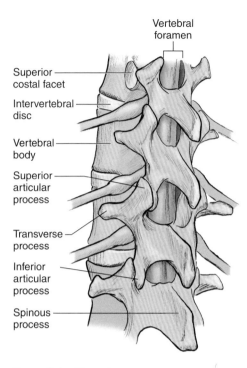

Figure 5.1 The spine.

Back Musculature

If you ride frequently, your back will become one of the most well-developed areas of your body. Multiple layers of muscles provide support for and movement of both the spine and the shoulders (see figure 5.2). The large, triangular trapezius is the outermost muscle. This muscle originates at the base of the skull and along the spine and travels across the back to insert in the scapula and clavicle. The trapezius performs multiple actions because of its large, fanned-out anatomy with fibers running in multiple directions. From a functional standpoint, the muscle can be divided into three sections:

Superior fibers: Scapular elevation and abduction (shrugging or lifting the shoulders)

Middle fibers: Scapular retraction (pulling the shoulder blades together at the midline)

Lower fibers: Scapular depression (pulling the shoulder blades downward)

Combination of fibers: Scapular rotation

The latissimus dorsi is another large, triangular muscle of the back. It originates along the lower spine and upper posterior ridge of the pelvis (iliac crest). At the opposite end of the muscle, the fibers come together to form a tough fibrous band (tendon) that inserts onto the upper portion of the humerus (near the insertion of the pectoralis major). Contraction of the latissimus dorsi pulls the humerus downward and backward, resulting in shoulder extension. This muscle also performs shoulder adduction (pulling the arm inward toward the body).

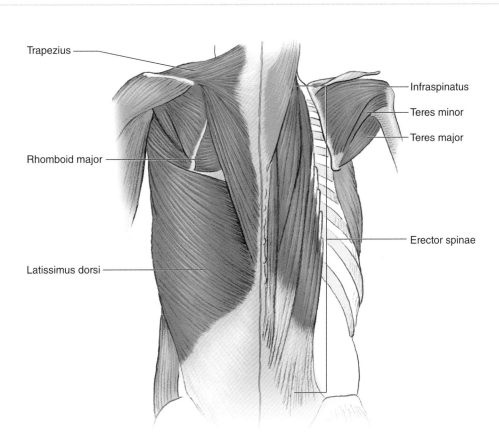

Figure 5.2   Muscles of the back.

Lying under the trapezius, the levator scapula, rhomboid major, and rhomboid minor connect the scapula to the upper spine. As the name implies, the levator scapula elevates the scapula. The rhomboid major and minor work in conjunction with the middle fibers of the trapezius to retract the scapula. All these muscles help stabilize the shoulder and the upper back.

The erector spinae muscles run along the length of the spinal column. Their primary role is stabilization and extension of the spine. When you hold your bent-over riding position on the bike, the erector spinae muscles contract and bear the brunt of the load. Many of the back exercises will either directly or indirectly train these vitally important muscles.

Warm-Up and Stretching

As mentioned in the previous chapters, a good warm-up is essential to preventing back injury. Riding a stationary bike is an effective way to warm up for the exercises in this chapter. Rowing is also a great cardio warm-up; it fires up your entire system while specifically warming the muscles of your back. Make sure you perform adequate stretching before getting into the exercises that follow. You can mimic some of the back exercises without using weights; you should hold each position for at least 30 seconds. You should also do some easy back bends and extension movements.

Seated Row

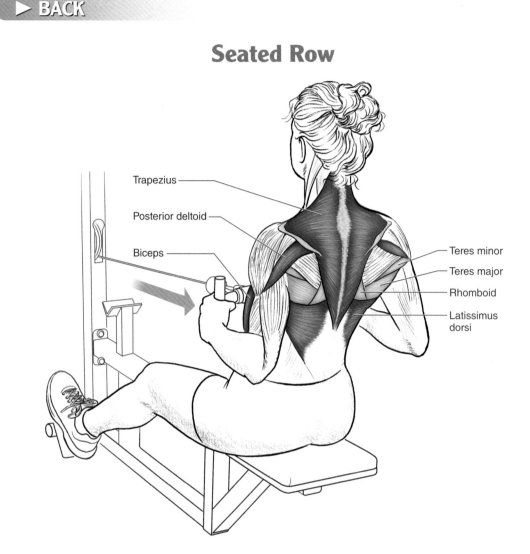

Trapezius

Posterior deltoid

Biceps

Teres minor

Teres major

Rhomboid

Latissimus dorsi

Execution

1. Place your feet shoulder-width apart on the rowing platform. Facing a low pulley, grip the handles using a thumbs-up grip. Your arms should be extended.

2. Keeping your back straight, concentrate on pulling your shoulder blades together, toward your spine. (Your arms should still be straight.)

3. Once your shoulder blades are retracted fully, pull the handle toward your chest, keeping your elbows tight to your sides.

4. Return to the starting position, first extending your arms and then letting your shoulder blades relax.

Muscles Involved

Primary: Trapezius, latissimus dorsi, posterior deltoid, biceps

Secondary: Rhomboid, teres major, teres minor, erector spinae, brachialis, brachioradialis

Cycling Focus

If you ride on varied terrain, at some point you'll inevitably encounter a steep section of road. Even in your bike's easiest gear, you can find yourself struggling to keep your forward momentum. Each turn of the pedals is a chore, and you'll have to rely on your arms and back to pull on the bars as you power through each rotation. The seated row exercise will help you develop adequate force in your arms and back. The grip position shown in the main illustration mimics holding your handlebars on the drops or hoods. Feel free to use a straight-bar attachment (grip with palms down) to mimic having your hands on the handlebar tops.

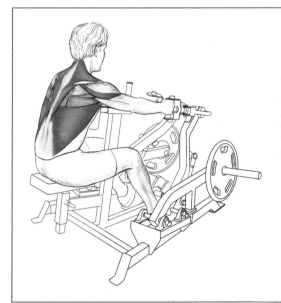

VARIATION

Machine Row

The machine row provides you with the same workout. However, you will lose some of the lower back workout because your chest is supported against the pad.

81

Shrug

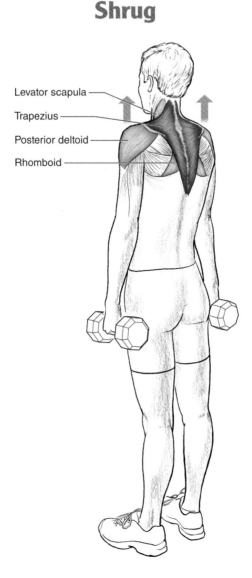

Levator scapula

Trapezius

Posterior deltoid

Rhomboid

Execution

1. Keeping your back straight and your arms extended, hold a dumbbell in each hand.
2. Without bending your arms, shrug your shoulders straight up toward your ears.
3. Slowly return to the starting position.

Muscles Involved

Primary: Trapezius

Secondary: Deltoid, levator scapula, erector spinae, forearms (grip strength)

Cycling Focus

Most of the muscles worked in this exercise are also used when you're leaning forward on your bike with your hands on the handlebars. These muscles will be under even greater stress when you start to climb out of the saddle. When standing, you'll lean forward, and more of your upper body weight will have to be supported by your shoulders and arms. You will also rely heavily on these muscles for support when you encounter rough roads. Although many cyclists never ride the old, cobbled roads of Europe, most will encounter plenty of construction zones and dilapidated country roads. With each jolt transferred from the road to your handlebars, your arms and shoulders will flex and contract to act as shock absorbers.

VARIATION

Barbell shrug: You can use a barbell instead of dumbbells for this exercise. Standing on stability disks while performing the exercise is a good way to increase the work for your legs, lower back, and torso.

Pull-Up

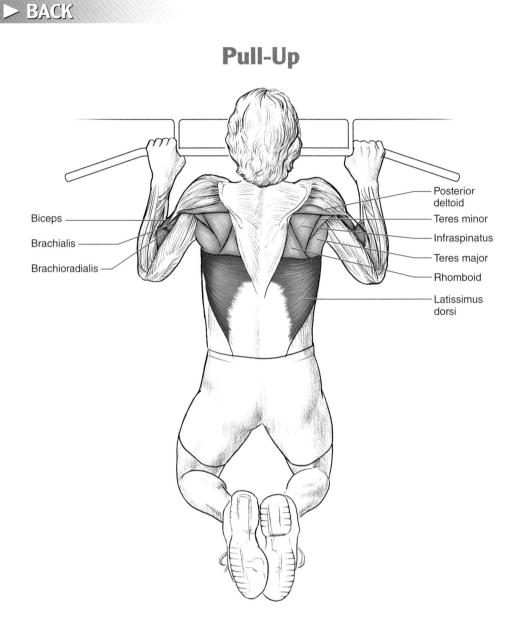

Biceps

Brachialis

Brachioradialis

Posterior deltoid

Teres minor

Infraspinatus

Teres major

Rhomboid

Latissimus dorsi

Execution

1. With your hands positioned slightly wider than shoulder-width apart, hang from the pull-up bar.
2. Without swinging, pull your chin up to the bar.
3. Slowly return to the starting position (arms extended).

Muscles Involved

Primary: Latissimus dorsi, biceps, brachialis, brachioradialis

Secondary: Posterior deltoid, rhomboid, teres major, teres minor, infraspinatus, external oblique, internal oblique, trapezius

Cycling Focus

This is a classic exercise that works most of the muscles in your back. It also places emphasis on the biceps, brachialis, and brachioradialis. As a cyclist, you'll rely on all these muscles to support your body and deliver the optimal drive to the cranks. Whether you're climbing, sprinting, or just cruising with your hands on the bars, some of the muscles trained in this exercise will be used. I like any exercise that works multiple muscle groups at the same time, and the straightforward pull-up definitely fits the bill. This exercise can be an effective part of almost any workout program.

VARIATION

Pull-up assist machine: This machine is a fantastic aid if you have difficulty performing an unassisted pull-up. The weight reading on the machine is the amount of aid provided during a pull-up. Hence, as you increase the amount of weight on the machine, the pull-up becomes easier.

Pull-Down

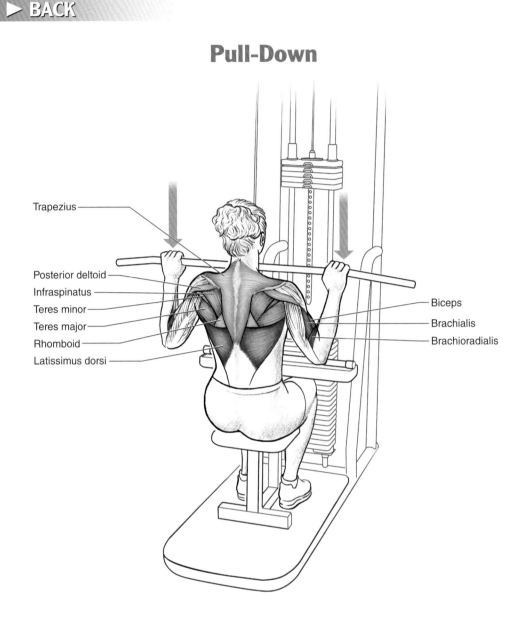

Trapezius

Posterior deltoid
Infraspinatus
Teres minor
Teres major
Rhomboid
Latissimus dorsi

Biceps
Brachialis
Brachioradialis

Execution

1. Sit with your thighs tucked under the pad. Use a wide, palm-out grip to grab the pull-down bar.
2. Keeping your body motionless, pull the bar downward until it touches your chest.
3. Return to the starting position (arms extended).

Muscles Involved

Primary: Latissimus dorsi, biceps, brachialis, brachioradialis

Secondary: Posterior deltoid, rhomboid, teres major, teres minor, infraspinatus, external oblique, internal oblique, trapezius

Cycling Focus

Like the pull-up, the pull-down is an exercise that gives you a lot of bang for your buck. The muscles of your back, arms, shoulders, and torso all contribute to the effort of this exercise. Having a strong back with good stability will keep you injury free and comfortable during training periods that involve heavy cycling. The off-season is a perfect time to bolster these muscles and prepare your body for the stress of the many miles to come. If your back is well prepared for the strain before your training season begins, you can focus on your fitness rather than back discomfort during the season.

VARIATION

Barbell Pull-Up

This exercise works many of the same muscles as the pull-down and pull-up. Because of the angle of movement, more emphasis will be placed on the posterior deltoid. Position the straight bar on a Smith machine at waist height. Hang under the bar with your arms extended and your torso straight. Your body should make a 45-degree angle with the floor. Looking toward the ceiling, pull your chest up to the bar. Slowly lower yourself and repeat.

Bent-Over Barbell Row

Trapezius
Posterior deltoid
Teres major
Rhomboid
Latissimus dorsi
Erector spinae

Execution

1. Hold the barbell using an overhand grip with your hands shoulder-width apart and your arms extended. Stand with your back leaning forward about 45 degrees to the floor.
2. Keeping your torso motionless, pull the barbell up vertically to your lower chest.
3. After a brief pause, lower the barbell to the starting position.

Muscles Involved

Primary: Latissimus dorsi

Secondary: Erector spinae, biceps, brachialis, brachioradialis, posterior deltoid, trapezius, rhomboid, teres major

Cycling Focus

From these illustrations, you can see that the position for this exercise closely resembles a common riding position. When riding up a climb with your hands on the hoods, you'll be pulling rhythmically on the bars. Your latissimus dorsi, shoulders, and arms will help provide stability and the extra drive you need to attack the climb. The bent-over barbell row is also ideal for the cyclist because it works the erector spinae. The angle used in this exercise is very close to your back's angle when you are on your bike and climbing out of the saddle.

By including this exercise in your training program, you'll be conditioned to withstand the grueling mountains ahead.

⚠️ **SAFETY TIP** You must be sure to bend only at the waist. Your spine should be straight. If you start to arch your back, you'll put unnecessary strain on your lower back. This may result in injury.

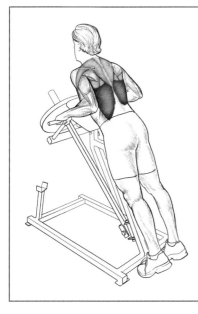

VARIATION

T-Bar Row

The T-bar row will give you added stability during the exercise. The lower back (erector spinae) will not be worked in this version of the exercise, but this can be beneficial if you're trying to overcome lower back soreness or injury.

Stability Ball Extension

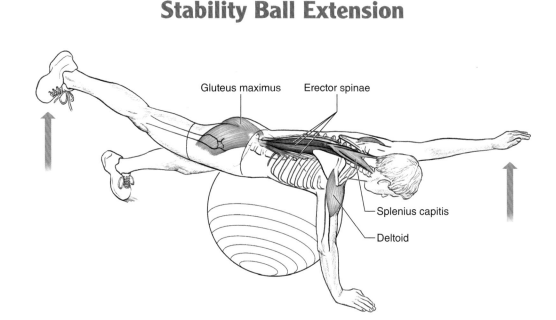

Gluteus maximus Erector spinae

Splenius capitis

Deltoid

Execution

1. Lie with your lower abdomen draped over a stability ball.
2. Keeping one foot on the floor, arch your back while raising and extending your arm and opposite leg. Your elbow and knee should be straight (extended).
3. Slowly lower your arm and leg. Curl your body around the stability ball.
4. Repeat the exercise using your other arm and leg.

Muscles Involved

Primary: Erector spinae

Secondary: Splenius capitis, gluteus maximus, deltoid

Cycling Focus

Your erector spinae muscles must withstand enduring workloads when you ride your bike. For the majority of your ride, these muscles will maintain your forward leaning posture. If your back becomes sore or fatigued, the erector spinae muscles are usually the culprit. The stability ball extension is particularly effective because it gives you full range of motion at maximal extension. This will counter the hours you'll spend with your back arched forward on the bike. Don't think that you need to use added weights to make this workout effective. Remember that stretching and moving your muscles through their complete range of motion will help you get the most out of your muscle fibers.

VARIATION

Same-side stability ball extension: A good variation is to raise the arm and leg on the same side rather than on opposite sides as described for the main exercise. This will stress different stabilizers and give you a well-rounded workout.

Reverse Leg Extension

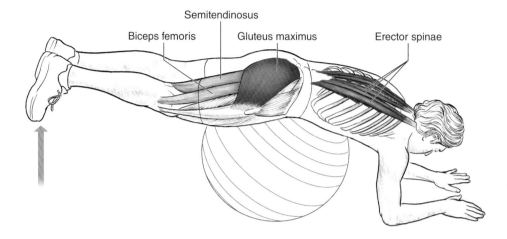

Semitendinosus

Biceps femoris   Gluteus maximus   Erector spinae

Execution

1. Lie with your lower abdomen on a stability ball. Extend both arms forward, and place your palms on the floor. Your legs should be straight, and your toes should be resting on the floor.
2. Keeping your knees straight, slowly extend at the hip, elevating your legs off the ground.
3. Return to the starting position.

Muscles Involved

Primary: Erector spinae, gluteus maximus

Secondary: Hamstrings

Cycling Focus

As previously mentioned, cycling is tough on your lower back. In the gym, you should focus on developing these back muscles in order to avoid future aggravation. The stability ball is an excellent tool because it allows freedom of motion with the added benefit of working all the stabilizer muscles. Remember, a balanced musculature is the key to proper alignment and injury prevention. Because you are so confined in position during your time on the bike, you should perform more range-of-motion exercises in the gym. You'll ride faster and better if your body is balanced and your muscles have strength through their entire spectrum of movement.

VARIATION

Incline Lumbar Extension

After you've been working this exercise for a while, you can hold weights to increase the difficulty. This exercise can also be done using an incline lumbar extension machine or bench. With the added stability, the workout for the stabilizer muscles is reduced.

Deadlift

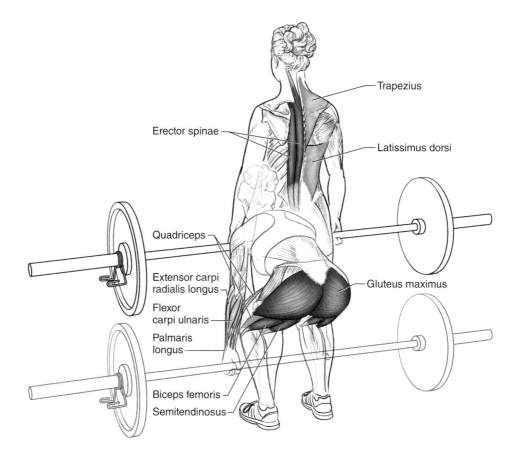

Trapezius

Erector spinae

Latissimus dorsi

Quadriceps

Extensor carpi radialis longus

Flexor carpi ulnaris

Palmaris longus

Gluteus maximus

Biceps femoris

Semitendinosus

Execution

1. Start with the barbell on the floor. Place your feet shoulder-width apart, and grab the barbell using an overhand, shoulder-width grip. Your arms will remain extended for the entire exercise.

2. Keeping your spine straight and your chin up, lift the barbell up to your waist, bending at the hips.

3. Slowly lower the weight back to the floor.

Muscles Involved

Primary: Erector spinae, gluteus maximus, hamstrings

Secondary: Trapezius, latissimus dorsi, quadriceps, forearms

Cycling Focus

As previously mentioned, the erector spinae muscles play a key role in the support of your body while you are on the bike. The deadlift exercise is great for cyclists because not only does it work these fundamental back muscles, but it also works some of the powerhouse muscles that help a cyclist power the cranks. The lower back clearly takes the load in this exercise, but you'll also get the benefit of strength training for the hamstrings, gluteals, and quadriceps. Again, I like exercises that work multiple muscles concurrently, and the deadlift definitely fits into this category.

⚠️ **SAFETY TIP** Correct form is a necessity during this exercise. Keep your head looking upward and your back straight. This will help straighten your spine and help you avoid injury.

VARIATION

Sumo Deadlift (Wide-Stance Deadlift)

Widen your stance and point your toes outward. Follow the same technique as described for the regular deadlift. You may want to use an over–under grip, as shown. By widening your stance, you'll emphasize training of the quadriceps and hip adductors.

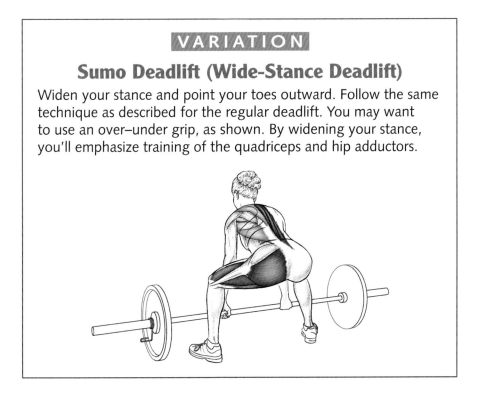

Good Morning

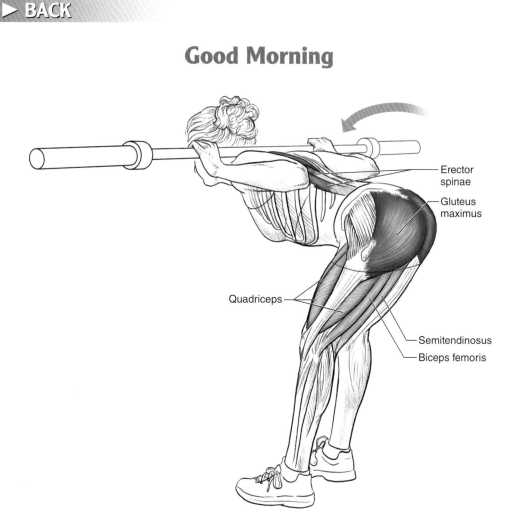

Erector spinae

Gluteus maximus

Quadriceps

Semitendinosus

Biceps femoris

Execution

1. With your feet shoulder-width apart, stand erect with a barbell across your shoulders.
2. Keeping your back straight and your eyes up, bend at the hips until your upper body is nearly parallel with the floor.
3. Slowly return your torso to the upright position.

Muscles Involved

Primary: Erector spinae, gluteus maximus

Secondary: Hamstrings, quadriceps

Cycling Focus

When performing this exercise, you must be careful not to overdo it and strain the muscles you are trying to train. The good morning will help develop the muscles that hold your posture while you're riding. Having strong erector spinae muscles will also improve your power delivery as well as your form. Ideally, your back should be fairly straight and flat when you are on your bike, with your

hands resting on the handlebar drops. Check your form on a trainer or when riding by a reflective window to make sure your back is flat and aerodynamic. Additionally, all the muscles running along your spine, including the erector spinae, will stabilize your spine and reduce the risk of vertebral subluxation (one vertebral body sliding forward onto another).

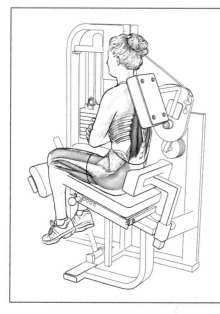

Machine Back Extension

When using the back extension machine, you'll have increased stability. If you've had back problems or if you are returning from a back injury, the machine is a good device for easing into a workout of the erector spinae muscles.

The abdominal muscles often don't receive enough attention from cyclists, but neglecting these muscles would be a big mistake. The abdominal muscles help establish your core strength, stability, and power. Training these muscles in the gym should be a key element in your weight training program. Strong abdominal muscles are fundamental to your fitness, performance, and overall health.

Low back pain in cyclists often results from the anterior muscles of the abdomen not being strong enough to counter the forceful back muscles. Because cyclists spend so much time leaning forward while in their riding position, they develop an amazingly strong and well-conditioned back. This hypertrophy (building) of the back is necessary and unavoidable when you spend a lot of time on the bike. However, the downside of this development is that it can throw off your spinal balance and skeletal stability.

As mentioned in chapter 5, your vertebrae should stack uniformly, one on top of the next. If your back muscles are pulling on your spine more than your anterior abdominal muscles are, your vertebrae will slowly be pulled out of alignment. If this misalignment progresses, your intervertebral discs may start to protrude. This is often referred to as a "slipped disc," and anyone who has experienced this unfortunate situation can attest to the high degree of discomfort and pain. This condition can become debilitating and may need to be repaired by a spinal surgeon. Ideally, with good conditioning and training as well as proper back care, you'll avoid this unpleasant experience. Adequate conditioning of your abdominal muscles needs to be done in the gym, and the core exercises in this chapter will show you proper form and training technique.

Another function of the abdominal muscles is to provide a stable platform for your two large pistons powering the cranks. As your legs rotate through the pedaling motion, your hip joint and pelvis are stabilized by your abdominal and back muscles. The foundation of any structure is fundamental to its stability, and your body is no different. To get the most drive from your legs to the pedals, your core needs to be solid and unwavering. This doesn't mean that your pelvis is not moving, but rather that your back and abdominal muscles are working in unison to provide the proper pelvic position during your pedal stroke. If your abdominal and back muscles are not locking your pelvis effectively, you will not be able to realize your optimal performance.

Finally, when you're riding at your limit and trying to suck every molecule of oxygen out of the air, your abdominal muscles will contribute to your maximal ventilatory (breathing) volume. As you strain under the high demands of your ride, your entire body will be working in concert to deliver sustained power to the pedals. Again, this is why conditioning and training your entire body will bring you the best results on the bike.

Abdominal Musculature

The abdominal muscles are a group of layered muscles that allow your torso to flex forward, rotate, and bend from side to side. In addition to the well-known rectus abdominis muscles (the "six pack"), three other muscles help form your abdominal wall. These muscles are positioned on top of each other, enabling them to efficiently provide the wide range of movement of your trunk. The exercises in this chapter will work all of these muscle groups.

The two side-by-side rectus abdominis muscles are the most visible and forward-facing muscles of the abdomen (see figure 6.1). They extend vertically from the lower margin of the ribs and sternum to the pubic bone of the pelvis. Surrounding these muscles is a tough fibrous material (fascia) called the rectus sheath. The rectus sheath creates a gridlike pattern that tacks down the muscle fibers. This forms both the central vertical demarcation down your abdomen (linea alba) and the horizontal divisions (tendinous inscription) that create the "six pack" appearance. The rectus abdominis muscles flex the torso forward. Working together, the upper muscles pull down on the ribs, and the lower muscles pull up on the pelvis. This performs the crunching motion used in many exercises.

The other three muscles of the abdomen are all lateral to the rectus abdominis. The outermost layer is the external oblique muscle. It is angled downward and inward from the ribs toward the linea alba and pelvis. As the muscle passes medially (inward), it forms a tough fibrous sheath called the external oblique aponeurosis. This coalesces into the rectus sheath mentioned previously.

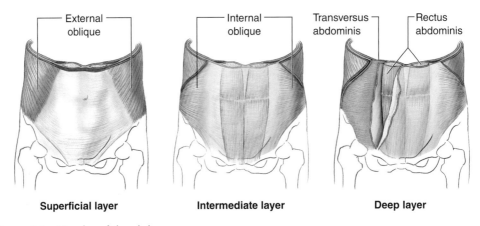

Superficial layer　　　**Intermediate layer**　　　**Deep layer**

Figure 6.1　Muscles of the abdomen.

The internal oblique is the middle layer of muscle. It is functionally angled in the opposite direction of the external oblique, running upward and inward from the pelvis toward the linea alba and ribs. The internal oblique also forms a fibrous aponeurosis that combines with the rectus sheath and the aponeurosis of the external oblique.

Contraction of both obliques on one side causes the torso to bend to that side. Simultaneous contraction of the obliques will aid the rectus abdominis in flexion. Bilateral contraction also protects and splints the abdominal wall whenever you're straining or bearing down (the Valsalva maneuver, or trying to push air out with a closed mouth and nose).

The innermost muscle is the transversus abdominis. As if designed by an engineer to cover all possible movements, the transversus abdominis runs horizontally from the back, ribs, and pelvis to the pubis and rectus sheath. Like the other abdominal muscles, it also forms fascia sheets. The thoracolumbar fascia of the back gives rise to the muscle laterally and medially (toward the center); the fascia contributes to the rectus sheath and abdominal aponeurosis. The primary role of the transversus abdominis is to help with forced expiration and increase intra-abdominal pressure. It also helps stabilize the abdominal wall during periods of high effort and strain.

This chapter provides exercises that will help you develop all your abdominal muscles. Anatomically, there is no upper, middle, and lower abdomen, but to help your focus in the gym, the exercises are divided into various abdominal sections. Although each exercise will work most of your abdominal muscles, certain areas will be under more stress and strain. As you perform each exercise, you should concentrate on those muscles described as "primary" in the exercise description. There is no quick way to achieve strong abdominal muscles—regardless of what some commercials might say! You have to spend time and effort in the gym to develop these important performance-enhancing muscles.

Warm-Up and Stretching

As with all workouts, you need to perform an adequate warm-up before engaging in these strenuous exercises. Spend 10 minutes doing cardio work on the exercise bike, treadmill, or elliptical. After you have elevated your heart rate and generated a sweat, you need to stretch the muscles of your abdomen and torso. Many of the exercise motions found in this chapter can serve as a good warm-up. Remove the resistance and perform the movement of the exercise as described. For the warm-up, you can slightly extend the range of motion compared to when doing the exercise with resistance. Here are two other good stretches:

1. Holding a broomstick across the back of your shoulders, twist at the torso from side to side for 30 to 60 seconds.
2. Stand erect with your feet together and your arms extended vertically above your head. Keeping your arms straight, extend and arch your back, reaching your hands upward and backward. Slowly arch your arms forward and downward, bending at the torso and keeping your legs straight. While keeping your legs straight, attempt to touch your toes. Reverse the motion until you return to your starting position. Repeat the complete range of motion until you feel adequately stretched.

Stability Ball Trunk Lift

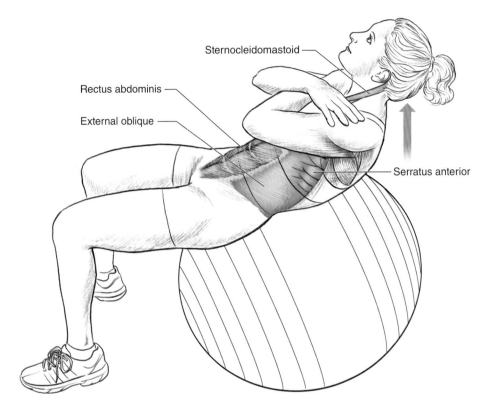

Sternocleidomastoid

Rectus abdominis

External oblique

Serratus anterior

Execution

1. Place your arms across your chest and rest your lower back on top of a stability ball. Your back and thighs should be horizontal and parallel with the floor. Your knees should be bent at 90 degrees, and your feet should be flat on the floor.
2. Lift your chin and torso upward as far as possible. Concentrate on moving your chin in a straight line toward the ceiling.
3. Pause briefly at your maximal height and then slowly return to the starting position.
4. For added difficulty, you can hold a medicine ball or weight plate with your arms outstretched over your chest throughout the entire motion.

Muscles Involved

Primary: Rectus abdominis (upper)

Secondary: Internal oblique, external oblique, serratus anterior, sternocleidomastoid

Cycling Focus

To deliver sustained power when riding your bike on a climb, you need to have a strong core that can handle the torque of your legs as they rotate through your pedal stroke. If you're delivering optimal power, you'll be pulling up with one leg while simultaneously crashing down with the other. At the same time, your arms will be pulling back and forth on the handlebars. Your core is the platform between your two sides, and the alternating movement of your legs and arms will naturally work to flex and destabilize your trunk. By maintaining a strong abdomen, you will help ensure that your upper body and pelvis can effectively fight against unnecessary movement. Any unwanted movement of your body or bike will lead to power loss and inefficiency. Even the best professionals only operate at near 27 percent efficiency, so saving your energy wherever possible is critical.

⚠ **SAFETY TIP** Keep your chin pointed upward toward the ceiling. Curling your chin down toward your chest will put undue strain on your cervical spine.

VARIATION

Side-to-Side Trunk Lift

Perform the same exercise, but instead of merely moving up and down, alternate lifting your body from side to side. This will not only work your rectus abdominis but will also focus on your obliques. Again, to increase the difficulty of the exercise, you can hold a medicine ball or weight with outstretched arms above your chest as you lift your trunk.

Stability Ball Pass

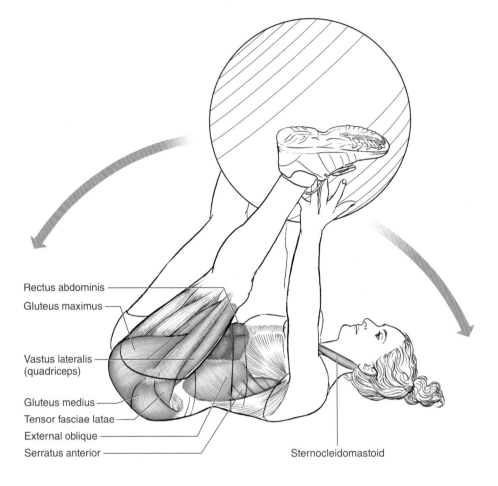

Rectus abdominis
Gluteus maximus
Vastus lateralis (quadriceps)
Gluteus medius
Tensor fasciae latae
External oblique
Serratus anterior
Sternocleidomastoid

Execution

1. Lie on your back with your legs extended. Squeeze a stability ball between your feet, and extend your arms horizontally above your head.
2. Perform a crunch motion, pulling your legs and arms to the vertical position. Your shoulders should come vertically off the floor.
3. Slowly return to the starting position.

Muscles Involved

Primary: Rectus abdominis (upper)

Secondary: External oblique, internal oblique, hip adductors, hip flexors, quadriceps, serratus anterior, sternocleidomastoid

Cycling Focus

The importance of pelvis stability when riding a bike cannot be overemphasized. Whether you're sprinting, climbing, or time trialing, your legs rely on a strong foundation to enable them to generate their impressive force while rotating the cranks. During a time trial, your body should be still and solid as you slice through the wind in your aerodynamic position. The more power you can deliver to the pedals, the faster you'll

ride. Your abdominal muscles will play a key role in establishing this needed base. The stability ball pass has the advantage of working some of your hip and leg muscles as well as your abdomen. By pushing your feet together to hold the ball, you will work your hip adductors. Good strength in both your adductors and abductors will help smooth your pedal stroke when you're fatigued or working at maximum capacity.

Rope Crunch

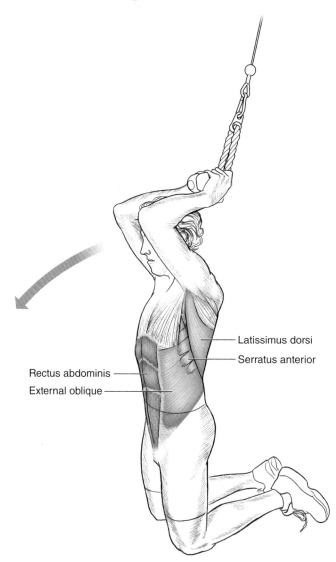

Latissimus dorsi

Serratus anterior

Rectus abdominis

External oblique

Execution

1. Facing away from the pulley system, kneel on a mat while holding a high pulley rope attachment above your head.
2. Curl your body downward toward the floor. Concentrate on bending at the waist.
3. Slowly return to the upright kneeling position.

Muscles Involved

Primary: Rectus abdominis (upper)

Secondary: External oblique, internal oblique, serratus anterior, latissimus dorsi

Cycling Focus

As previously discussed, the standard cycling position places an immense amount of strain on your back. All the hypertrophy of the back that results from hours of riding will need to be balanced by abdominal muscle training. Rope crunches will help keep your spine in good alignment as well as produce a solid core. The end of this exercise places you in a similar position to being in your drops on the bike. It therefore works the abdominal muscles where needed the most. As you move through the range of motion of this exercise, you should try to feel how it mimics various positions on the bike (hoods, tops, drops, time trialing). This will help train your body's awareness of position and focus the exercise on areas that need the most stabilization.

VARIATION

Floor crunch: Lie with your back flat on a mat. Lift your thighs so they are vertical (perpendicular to the floor). Perform a crunching motion, concentrating on lifting your chin and shoulders straight up in the air.

Stability Ball Pike

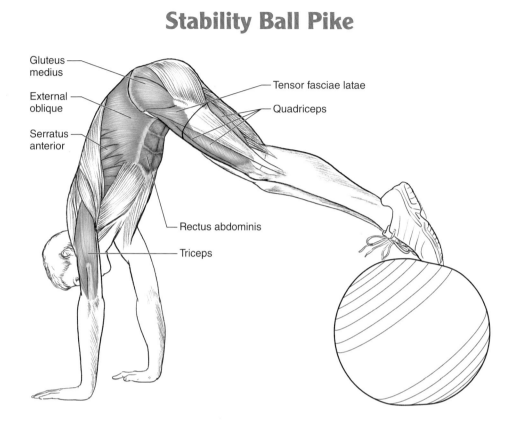

Gluteus medius

External oblique

Serratus anterior

Tensor fasciae latae

Quadriceps

Rectus abdominis

Triceps

Execution

1. Get into a push-up position with your shins on top of a stability ball.
2. Lift your waist upward, rolling the ball toward your head as far as possible.
3. Keep your back and legs straight during the entire exercise.
4. Return to the starting position.

Muscles Involved

Primary: Rectus abdominis (middle)

Secondary: External oblique, internal oblique, serratus anterior, hip flexors, quadriceps, triceps

Cycling Focus

This exercise is terrific for cyclists. It works core stability as well as the abdominal muscles, quadriceps, arms, and shoulders. Because the ball can freely roll, you will be forced to use all of your accessory stabilizing muscles to maintain good form. These are the same muscles that will help you with your riding form when you become fatigued. When riding, your key foundation points will be your arms on the handlebars and your feet on the pedals. This exercise trains the same muscles. You'll be amazed at how tough this exercise

is, and you'll definitely notice your gains once you hit the road. Focus on controlled inhalation and exhalation throughout the entire range of motion. When riding your bike, you must continue controlled breathing even during tough efforts. Without the delivery of new oxygen to the muscles—and the removal of carbon dioxide from the muscles—you'll soon lose power and the ability to rotate the cranks.

Plank

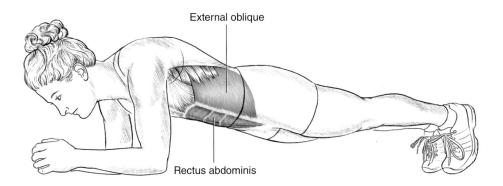

External oblique

Rectus abdominis

Execution

1. Using your forearms rather than your hands, get into a standard push-up position.
2. Keep your back straight. Hold the position for 30 seconds to 1 minute.
3. Rest for 30 seconds to 1 minute and then repeat.

Muscles Involved

Primary: Rectus abdominis (middle)

Secondary: External oblique, internal oblique

Cycling Focus

If you have to watch TV, then this is the way to do it! To make good use of your time, you should try this exercise the next time you find yourself in front of the tube. As with the other abdominal exercises, this one helps build a strong foundation on which to base your power when riding. This exercise causes you to splint your abdominal wall. This will help strengthen the respiratory muscles that maximally will deliver oxygen to your lungs when you're really putting the hammer down. As your fitness improves, you can increase the time that you hold the position.

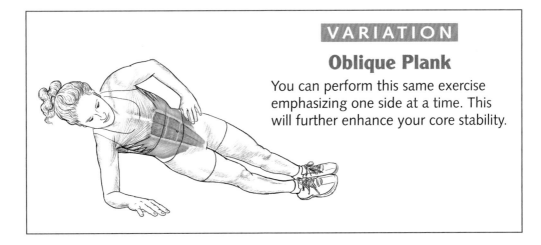

VARIATION

Oblique Plank

You can perform this same exercise emphasizing one side at a time. This will further enhance your core stability.

Reverse Crunch

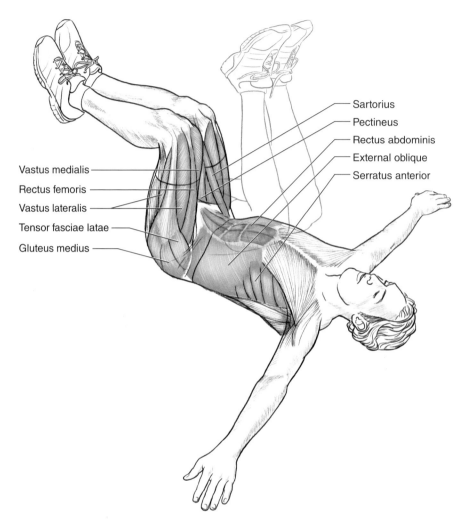

Sartorius
Pectineus
Rectus abdominis
External oblique
Serratus anterior

Vastus medialis
Rectus femoris
Vastus lateralis
Tensor fasciae latae
Gluteus medius

Execution

1. Lie with your back flat on the floor, your arms extended outward, and your knees bent at 90 degrees. Your thighs should be vertical with a 90-degree bend at the hip.

2. Focus on lifting your pelvis upward off the floor and bringing your knees toward your chest. Your lower legs will become vertical and perpendicular to the floor.

3. Slowly lower your legs and pelvis to the starting position.

Muscles Involved

Primary: Rectus abdominis

Secondary: External oblique, internal oblique, transversus abdominis, serratus anterior, quadriceps, hip flexors

Cycling Focus

The reverse crunch focuses on your lower abdominal muscles. This is exactly where you need the most solid foundation during your rides. Your powerful legs need these muscles to remain steadfast during extreme efforts. Imagine being in a two-man breakaway as you near the finish. Each of you rotates through, breaking

the wind and trying to keep the pace high. You maintain as aerodynamic a position as possible, and your legs are pulling hard. Luckily, your training helps keep your pelvis stable. As you pull off, you'll have to quickly recover from your effort before you need to drive on again. This will require forceful blowing off of your carbon dioxide. Your obliques and transversus abdominis will be working overtime to help provide maximal ventilation.

Hanging Knee Raise

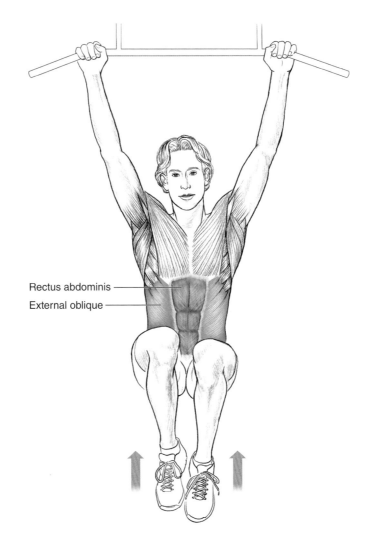

Rectus abdominis

External oblique

Execution

1. Hang from the pull-up bar using a palm-forward grip.
2. Simultaneously lift both knees until your thighs are parallel with the floor.
3. After a brief pause in the up position, slowly lower your legs back down.

Muscles Involved

Primary: Rectus abdominis

Secondary: External oblique, internal oblique, transversus abdominis, hip flexors

Cycling Focus

This exercise not only works your abdominal muscles, but also stretches and decompresses your spine. After long rides, it always feels good to get in the gym and perform this exercise. Sitting on the saddle compresses your spine, and the forward leaning position on the bike can tighten your back muscles. Before and after a set of hanging knee raises, you should hang for a few moments to let the ligaments and muscles get a good stretch. As you lift your legs, you'll feel the strain on your abdominal muscles. This exercise will give you a great workout to help balance the power of your lower back. You'll also be training your smaller stabilizers if you keep your body under control during the exercise—no swinging as you lift and lower your legs. In addition, you'll be working your forearms and grip strength by hanging from the bar. If you have trouble holding on to the bar for the entire set, try using the arm slings. Slip your hand and elbow through the sling and let your body weight rest on the back of your upper arms.

VARIATION

Alternating hanging knee raise: Instead of raising your legs straight up in front, try doing a set in which you alternate raising your knees to one side and then the other. This will place added emphasis on your oblique muscles.

Stability Ball V

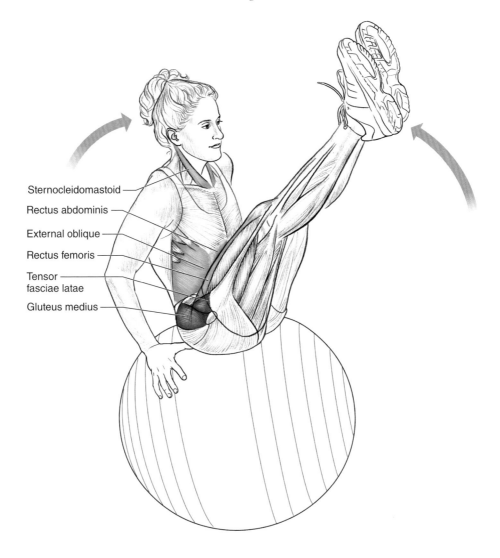

Sternocleidomastoid

Rectus abdominis

External oblique

Rectus femoris

Tensor
fasciae latae

Gluteus medius

Execution

1. Sit on a large stability ball, placing your hands behind and to the side of your buttocks. Lean your torso back slightly and hold your feet off the ground, keeping your legs straight.
2. Create a "V" with your body by bending at the hips. Keep your knees and torso straight.
3. Slowly bring your torso and legs together, decreasing the angle of the V.
4. Return to the starting position.

Muscles Involved

Primary: Rectus abdominis, hip flexors

Secondary: External oblique, internal oblique, rectus femoris, sternocleidomastoid

Cycling Focus

The stability ball V is a tough exercise. It requires strength, coordination, balance, and focus—all of which will help your riding. Because you keep your legs and torso straight—only bending at the hips—you'll condition and strengthen the linkage between your upper and lower body. The hip flexors get a great workout, and the power gained from this exercise will be directly applicable to your riding. By using the stability ball, you'll get a lot of work out of your hips, pelvis, and trunk stabilizers. This will help solidify your skeletal foundation and give you a great platform for delivering optimal power to the pedals.

VARIATION

Bench V: If you have a difficult time performing the exercise on a stability ball, you can use the same technique while sitting on a flat workout bench. After you master the exercise on a stable platform, you'll likely be able to move to the stability ball. (Don't feel bad if you initially have trouble with the stability ball. It's hard!)

Trunk Twist

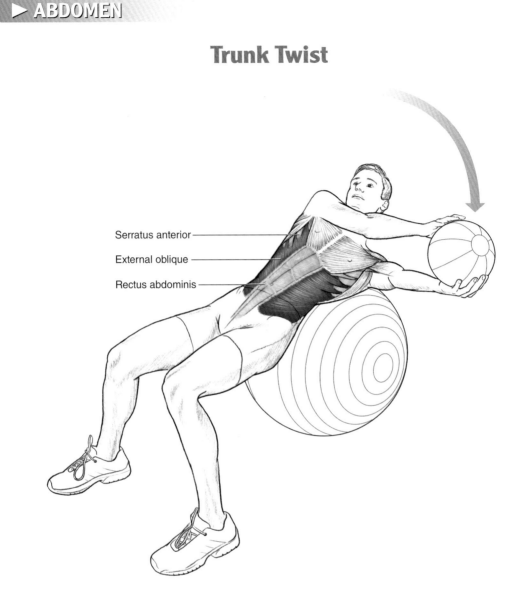

Serratus anterior

External oblique

Rectus abdominis

Execution

1. Lie with the middle of your back resting on a large stability ball. With extended arms, hold a medicine ball or weight plate vertically above your chest.
2. Keeping your elbows straight, sweep your arms to the left until they are nearly parallel with the ground.
3. Return your arms to the starting (vertical) position and repeat the movement to the other side.

Muscles Involved

Primary: Internal oblique, external oblique

Secondary: Rectus abdominis, serratus anterior, sternocleidomastoid

Cycling Focus

If you watch professional riders climb out of the saddle, you'll notice how still they keep their upper body. Even when they are going all out and powerfully turning the cranks, they maintain a calm composure. The obliques trained in the trunk twist exercise are key in providing that stability. With each turn of the pedal, the bike wants to rock from side to side. To prevent this movement, your internal and external obliques, transversus abdominis, and rectus abdominis will all be firing to lock down your torso. When the going gets rough, these muscles will also help you achieve your maximum respiratory effort to keep the engine churning.

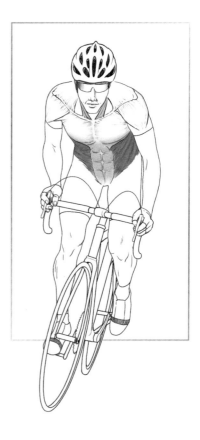

VARIATION

Broomstick Twist

The broomstick twist is a great exercise for increasing flexibility and working out any kinks or tight spots in your torso. You can use a simple broomstick or a weighted bar (these bars are found in many gyms). Focus on complete range of motion.

Oblique Crunch

Serratus anterior

Rectus abdominis

External oblique

Execution

1. Lie with your side resting on a large stability ball, your hands on the sides of your head, and your elbows pulled back.
2. Lower your trunk downward, wrapping your side around the ball.
3. Slowly raise your trunk by lifting your upward-facing elbow toward the sky.
4. After the set, repeat on the other side.

Muscles Involved

Primary: Internal oblique, external oblique

Secondary: Rectus abdominis, serratus anterior

Cycling Focus

Whether you're lifting weights or sprinting on a bike, your abdominal muscles will be contracting to splint your abdominal wall. The Valsalva maneuver (trying to push air out with a closed mouth and nose) makes your torso firm and rigid. This protects your spine and abdominal contents, and it helps deliver optimal force to your endeavor. The next time you engage in a full-power sprint or acceleration, note the firmness of your entire abdomen. The oblique crunch exercise will help train this musculature and help prevent injuries such as a hernia or back strain.

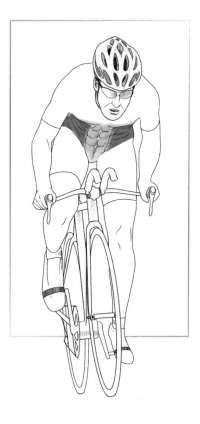

Incline Oblique Crunch

Position yourself so that the side of one of your hips is resting against the pad on an incline roman chair. Your feet should be side by side and wedged under the foot pad. Hold a dumbbell with your arm hanging straight downward. The other arm should be bent at the elbow with your hand resting on the back of your head. Bend sideways toward your downward hip, and lower the weight toward the floor. Slowly return to the starting position. To isolate the sideways movement, make sure you do not bend forward or backward at the waist.

CHAPTER 7

LEGS: MUSCLE ISOLATION

The legs and hips are the fundamental driving force of the cyclist. Like the well-defined muscles of a thoroughbred racehorse, the legs on a cyclist display years of hard training and conditioning. Professional cyclists treat their legs like a valuable commodity. Not only do they focus on developing strength and power in the gym, but they also ensure proper recovery after training. Stretching, compression stockings, massage, and elevation are all utilized to avoid injury and get the most out of their workouts.

Throughout the previous chapters, we've discussed the importance of the body's other musculature to the rider's performance. But no muscle group is as important to the cyclist as the lower extremities. With all the other muscles of the body playing the role of supporting cast, the legs are unquestionably the stars of the show. The rider's entire body revolves around the primary purpose of delivering optimal power to the cranks. The exercises in this chapter will guide you to greater strength and fitness in your lower extremities—and thus show you the road to improved cycling performance.

Because of the importance of the lower extremities, cyclists sometimes focus all their workout time on this area of the body. However, you must not forget about all the exercises for the muscles discussed in the previous chapters. Remember, the best quarterback would be useless without all the supporting teammates who allow him to do his job. The same can be said for your legs. Without support and a firm foundation, your legs will never be able to perform at their maximum potential.

Skeletal Anatomy

The three major joints of the lower body are the hip, knee, and ankle. The hip is a ball-and-socket joint that articulates (connects) the proximal end of the femur to the pelvis. The top part of the femur, known as the femoral head, forms the "ball." The "socket" is formed by the acetabulum of the pelvis. A ball-and-socket joint allows a wide range of flexibility and movement. Although the hip can move in six different directions, the cyclist primarily uses the two most powerful movements—flexion (moving the knee up during the up pedal stroke) and extension (moving the knee down during the down pedal stroke). The hip can also move in adduction (pulling the leg inward), abduction (moving the leg outward to the side), internal rotation (turning the foot inward), and external rotation (turning the foot outward).

The knee joint is formed by three bones: the femur (positioned superiorly), the tibia (positioned inferiorly), and the patella (kneecap). As a hinge joint, the knee's range of motion is more limited than the hip's. It moves in only one plane, performing flexion (bending the knee) and extension (straightening the knee). Multiple ligaments stabilize the knee joint under force. These ligaments include the medial collateral ligament (MCL), lateral collateral ligament (LCL), anterior cruciate ligament (ACL), and posterior cruciate ligament (PCL).

The ankle also works as a hinged joint, but it is much more complicated than the knee. Actually, two different joints are often collectively referred to as the "ankle." The true ankle joint is composed of the tibia, fibula, and talus. The combined position of the tibia and fibula forms a snug cap that rests on top of the rectangular surface of the talus. This joint moves in the vertical plane, in both dorsiflexion (foot up) and plantar flexion (foot down). The calcaneotalar joint is the second of the two joints; as the name implies, this joint is composed of the calcaneus and talus. This joint enables the foot to move in inversion (rolling the foot inward) and eversion (rolling the foot outward). Multiple ligaments, including the lateral ligament complex and the medial deltoid ligament, stabilize the entire ankle and the calcaneotalor joint, making them extremely tough and stable.

Quadriceps

The quadriceps muscle performs extension of the knee and becomes highly developed and powerful in most cyclists. Four different muscle bellies make up the quadriceps muscle:

1. Rectus femoris
2. Vastus intermedius
3. Vastus medialis
4. Vastus lateralis

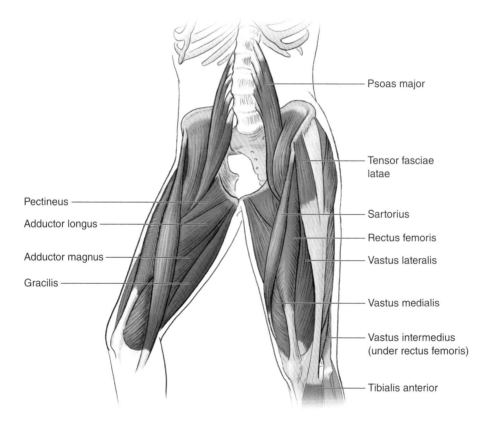

Figure 7.1   Muscles of the front of the leg.

These muscle bellies all come together as they cross over the knee to form a fibrous band that engulfs the patella. This fibrous band is known as the patellar tendon, and its insertion is on the anterior (front) of the proximal end of the tibia. The rectus femoris originates on the iliac spine of the pelvis. The vastus lateralis, vastus intermedius, and vastus medialis originate on the lateral, anterior, and medial surfaces of the upper femur. See figure 7.1 for an illustration of these muscles.

Hamstrings

The hamstring is the large posterior (back) muscle group of the upper leg (see figure 7.2). This muscle group acts as the primary flexor of the knee. The hamstring group is formed by three muscles:

1. Biceps femoris
2. Semimembranosus
3. Semitendinosus

The hamstring originates on the ischial tuberosity of the pelvis and the posterior aspect of the femur. The muscle tracts down the back of the femur and inserts on the lateral and medial condyles of the tibia as well as on the fibular head. Because the hamstring spans both the hip and knee joint, it has a dual action. The hamstring performs knee flexion and also acts as a hip extender. Similar to the quadriceps, the hamstring becomes a powerful muscle in the well-developed cyclist.

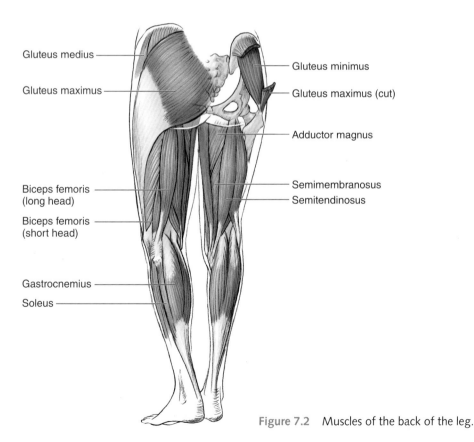

Figure 7.2 Muscles of the back of the leg.

Gluteals

The gluteus maximus is the largest and most apparent gluteal muscle (see figure 7.2). This muscle is the primary hip extensor, and it gives the cyclist serious downward power during the pedal cycle. The gluteus maximus originates on the ilium and sacrum of the pelvis. It runs medial to lateral (inside to out) and inserts on the femur. Along with the tensor fasciae latae, the gluteus maximus contributes to the iliotibial (IT) band. This thick fibrous sheath travels down the lateral part of the thigh to insert on the lateral condyle of the tibia. The IT band is often the cause of discomfort after hard training days.

The two other gluteal muscles—the gluteus minimus and gluteus medius—act as rotational and lateral movers of the leg. The gluteus minimus abducts and internally rotates the thigh. This muscle lies underneath the gluteus maximus and connects the pelvis to the greater trochanter of the femur. The gluteus medius also abducts the thigh. Depending on the degree of abduction, the gluteus medius can either internally or externally rotate the leg.

Other Upper Leg Muscles

Numerous other muscles help the hip move in both adduction (toward the centerline) and abduction (away from the centerline):

Hip adductors: Gracilis, adductor brevis, adductor longus, adductor magnus, pectineus

Hip abductors: Gluteus medius, gluteus minimus, tensor fasciae latae, sartorius

The hip flexors are not nearly as powerful as the gluteus maximus discussed above. However, as mentioned elsewhere in this book, the goal of an efficient cyclist is to have a smooth, constant pedal stroke. Therefore, cyclists should train not only the hip extenders, but also the following group of hip flexors:

Hip flexors: Sartorius, iliopsoas, rectus femoris, tensor fasciae latae, pectineus, adductor brevis, adductor longus

Lower Leg Musculature

The posterior muscles of the lower leg are also very important to the cyclist. The three muscle bellies of the calf—medial gastrocnemius, lateral gastrocnemius, and soleus—are collectively called the triceps surae (see figure 7.2 on page 125). All of these muscles help the cyclist perform plantar flexion, which is an important part of the pedaling motion. The gastrocnemius originates on the medial and lateral condyle of the femur and inserts on the calcaneus (heel bone) via the Achilles tendon. Because it crosses the knee joint, it also aids the hamstring in knee flexion. The soleus originates on both the tibia and fibula. Along with the gastrocnemius, the soleus inserts onto the calcaneus by way of the Achilles tendon.

The anterior (front) compartment of the lower leg houses numerous muscles that perform dorsiflexion (upward foot and toe movement). The tibialis anterior is the medial (middle) muscle, and it extends from the lateral condyle of the tibia to the first metatarsal and first cuneiform bone of the foot. During the pedal stroke, you'll activate this muscle to pull your foot upward. Other muscles in this area include the extensor hallucis longus (dorsiflexion of the great toe), the extensor digitorum longus (dorsiflexion of the toes), and the peroneus tertius (dorsiflexion and eversion of the foot). The peroneus longus and brevis are found in the lateral compartment of the lower leg and primarily act to evert the ankle.

The exercises in this chapter will help you isolate the various leg muscles that you'll use while riding. By focusing your training on specific muscles, you'll be able to strengthen the foundation on which you build your riding power. The next two chapters will provide exercises for working multiple muscle groups at the same time. During these combination exercises, your body can sometimes "cheat" and use stronger muscles to support and help weaker muscles. That's why isolation exercises are so crucial to your training.

Warm-Up and Stretching

The legs contain large muscle groups, so you must adequately warm up extensive muscle tissue before doing a leg workout. Spend 10 minutes riding the stationary bike before stretching. You need to stretch each major muscle group. You should perform exercises that specifically stretch the quadriceps, hamstrings, gluteals, and calves before any resistance training. This may seem a bit tedious and time consuming, but it is very important for helping you avoid injury.

Leg Extension

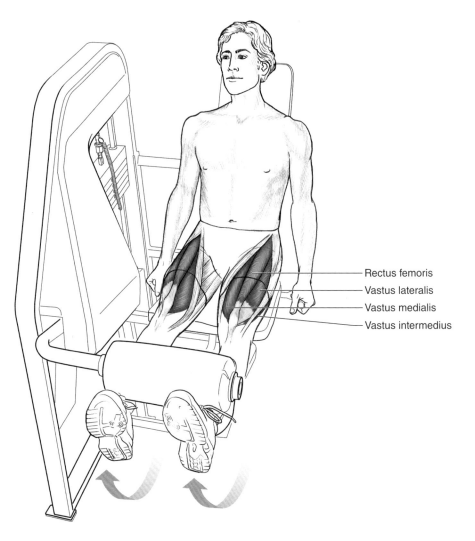

Rectus femoris
Vastus lateralis
Vastus medialis
Vastus intermedius

Execution

1. Sit on the machine with the middle of your knee aligned with the pivot point.
2. Raise your legs until your knees are straight. Your toes should be pointed upward.
3. After a brief pause, return to the starting position (knees bent to 90 degrees).

Muscles Involved

Primary: Quadriceps

Secondary: None

Cycling Focus

The next time you go out on a ride, try to feel your various leg muscles firing while you are pedaling at a steady rate. Try to do the same during a fierce acceleration in a sprint or a climb. You'll note that as your leg kicks over the top of the pedal stroke, your quadriceps will fire with a vengeance. You'll also be able to feel the similarity between this part of your pedaling motion and the motion used on the leg extension machine. This exercise (like the others in this chapter) isolates one of your major cycling muscles. Look at the development of any serious rider's quads, and you'll realize just how much these muscles are used during riding.

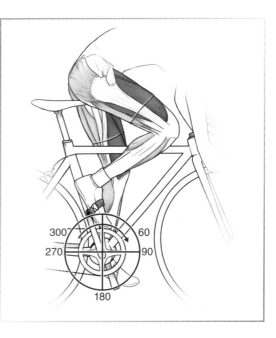

⚠ SAFETY TIP To avoid lower back injury, keep your spine flat against the machine pad.

Seated Leg Curl

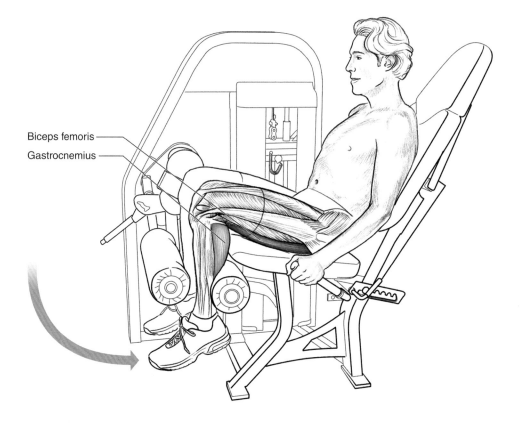

Biceps femoris
Gastrocnemius

Execution

1. Sit on the machine with the middle of your knee aligned with the pivot point.
2. Keeping your back flat, flex at the knees until they are bent to 90 degrees. Keep your toes pointed upward.
3. After a brief pause, return to the starting position (knees straight).

Muscles Involved

Primary: Hamstrings

Secondary: Gastrocnemius, gracilis, sartorius, popliteus

Cycling Focus

The efficiency of the pedal stroke requires the constantly alternating and combined effort of both your legs. As one leg is emphasizing pulling, the other is emphasizing pushing. Just as the leg extension exercise replicates the top and front part of your pedal stroke, the leg curl focuses on the bottom and back part of your pedaling motion. As you sit on the leg curl machine, imagine pulling your foot through the bottom arc of your pedal stroke. Feel the similarity between the exercise motion and the upward pull you perform when completing a revolution of the

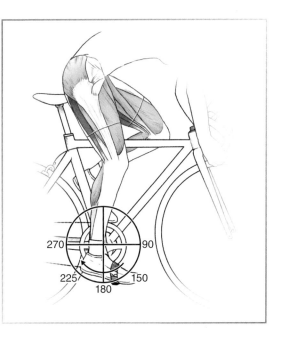

crank. Be sure you don't "cheat" on this exercise by arching your back and angling your hips. Remember, the purpose is to isolate the hamstrings and give them the best training possible.

VARIATION

Lying Leg Curl

The lying leg curl also incorporates a slight hip extension when maximally contracting your hamstrings.

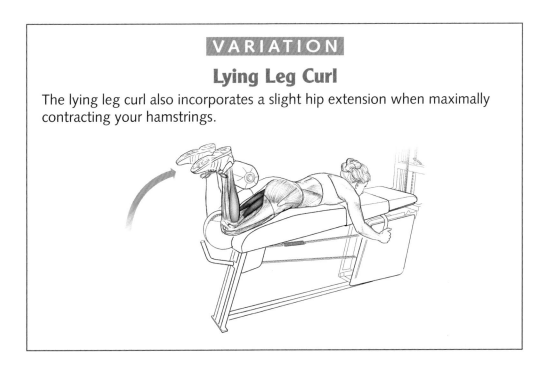

Stiff-Leg Deadlift

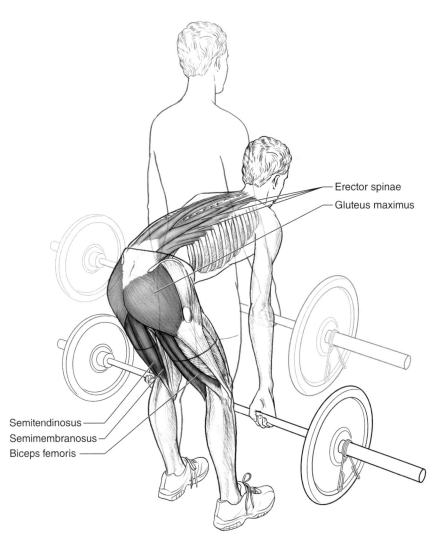

Erector spinae
Gluteus maximus
Semitendinosus
Semimembranosus
Biceps femoris

Execution

1. Stand with your feet shoulder-width apart. Hold the bar using a shoulder-width, palm-down grip. Your arms should be straight.
2. Bend forward at the waist, keeping your back and legs straight.
3. After nearly touching the floor with the weights, return to the starting (upright) position.

Muscles Involved

Primary: Hamstrings

Secondary: Erector spinae, gluteus maximus

Cycling Focus

The stiff-leg deadlift focuses on the entire back side of the rider's physique. During the exercise, you can really feel how this replicates the movement of your legs when you're bent forward in your handlebar drops or aero bars. If you focus on your back, hips, and thighs while riding—and then recall the sensation while performing the stiff-leg deadlift—you'll see the benefit of working this exercise in the gym. A large portion of your power on the bike, whether you are sitting or standing, comes from the extension of your leg at the hip. When you focus on this area in your workout, you will definitely reap the benefits in your power and performance.

⚠ **SAFETY TIP** Make certain to keep your head up. This will help keep your spine straight and prevent low back injury.

VARIATION

Dumbbell stiff-leg deadlift: If you have a difficult time managing the bar, you can perform the exercise using dumbbells. Follow the same form as described for the stiff-leg deadlift.

Standing Calf Raise

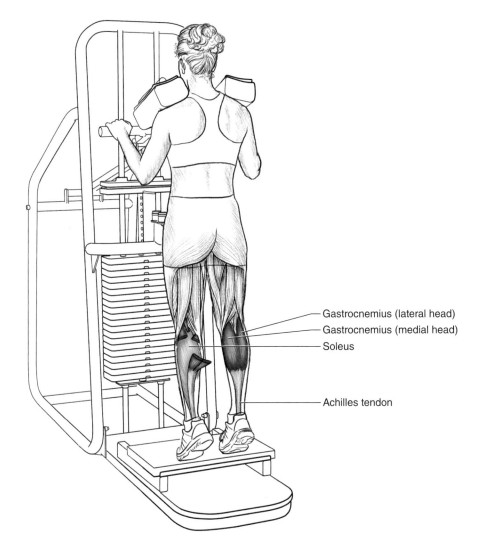

Gastrocnemius (lateral head)
Gastrocnemius (medial head)
Soleus

Achilles tendon

Execution

1. Place your toes on the platform, and place your shoulders snugly under the pads.
2. Keeping your back and knees straight, lower your heels until you feel a good stretch in your calves.
3. Slowly raise your body by raising your heels to the tiptoe position.
4. Return to the starting (heel down) position.

Muscles Involved

Primary: Gastrocnemius

Secondary: Soleus

Cycling Focus

The calf is a highly developed muscle on any serious cyclist. As your leg moves through the pedaling motion, your gastrocnemius and soleus will add to the power of each rotation. To maintain efficiency, the angle of your foot in relation to the ground should not be changing drastically during the rotation of the pedals. Since the crank is constantly moving, your ankle must act as a buffer to keep your foot in its relatively stable position. The gastrocnemius and soleus play a big part in this movement at the ankle. Whenever

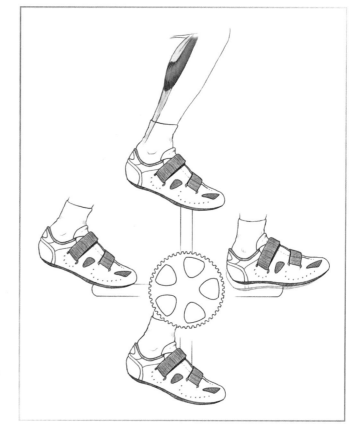

you move your leg downward through the pedaling stroke, your gastrocnemius and soleus will contribute to the downward force transferred to the pedal—and subsequently to the forward progress of the bike. When I was racing, I used to study the pedal rotation and foot position of Andy Hampsten. His efficient pedaling motion is a perfect example of proper foot position and ankle movement.

Seated Reverse Calf Press

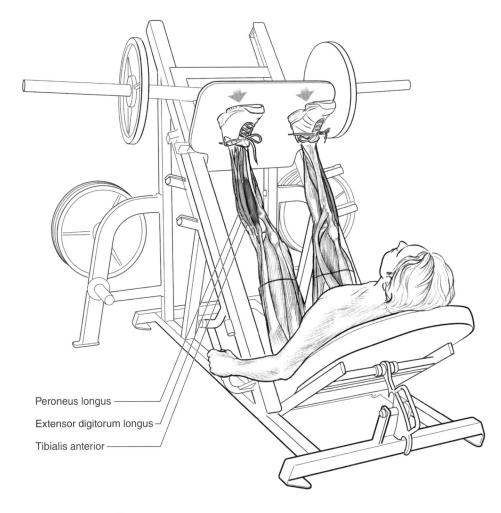

Peroneus longus

Extensor digitorum longus

Tibialis anterior

Execution

1. Place your feet high on the platform of the leg press.
2. Keeping your knees straight, pull the tops of your feet back toward your body while pushing the platform with your heels.
3. Return to the starting position (feet fully resting on the platform).

Muscles Involved

Primary: Tibialis anterior

Secondary: Extensor digitorum longus, peroneus longus

Cycling Focus

Efficiency is a key component to being a successful cyclist. Ideally, any effort or movement of the rider should make the bike move forward faster. Unfortunately, a good portion of a cyclist's effort is often lost in translation, whether it's because of wind resistance, heat dissipation, equipment issues, or other factors. So every little bit of power generation and efficient movement helps. As previously mentioned, the foot should remain relatively still during the pedaling motion. Like the gastrocnemius and soleus, the anterior muscles of the lower leg also contribute to this stability. These anterior muscles also help drive the pedal upward during the back half of the pedal stroke. The seated reverse calf press will help isolate these muscles and specifically prepare them to do their part during your pedal stroke.

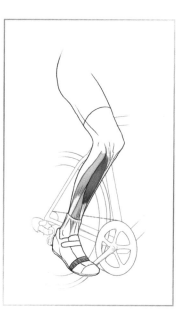

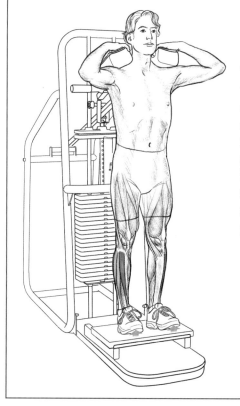

VARIATION

Standing Reverse Calf Raise

You can work the anterior muscles of the lower leg using various machines. If you'd prefer not to switch, you can work these muscles on the same machine used in the calf raise. Turn around and face outward, placing your heels on the platform. Lift your toes upward, completing the same motion as described for the seated reverse calf press.

Machine Adduction

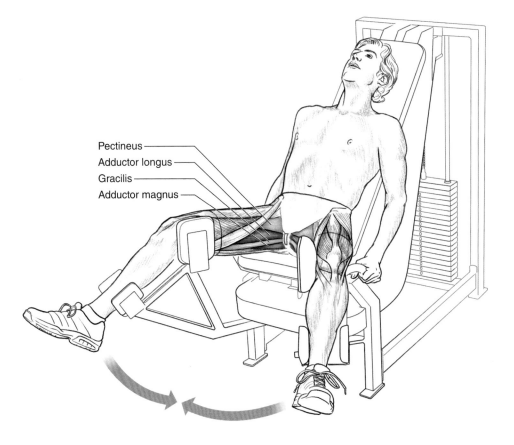

Pectineus
Adductor longus
Gracilis
Adductor magnus

Execution

1. Sit on the adduction machine with your legs spread.
2. Slowly bring your legs together until the leg pads touch.
3. With controlled movement, bring your legs back to the starting position.

Muscles Involved

Primary: Adductor magnus, adductor longus

Secondary: Gracilis, pectineus, lower gluteus maximus

Cycling Focus

Although you won't actually move your legs in adduction during your pedaling motion, you still need to strengthen the adductor muscles. During hard efforts, you'll want to maintain a clean, streamlined rotational motion of your legs. Your adductors will help support the primary movers of the cranks. By conditioning your adductors, you can decrease the likelihood of your form breaking down when you are fatigued. If you watch a professional's pedaling motion—even at the end of the race when the rider is tired—you'll notice how smoothly the legs rotate. This comes from years of training and from having well-conditioned accessory muscles that help keep the legs properly aligned.

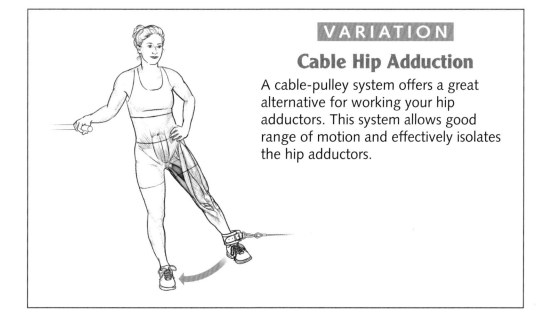

VARIATION

Cable Hip Adduction

A cable-pulley system offers a great alternative for working your hip adductors. This system allows good range of motion and effectively isolates the hip adductors.

Machine Abduction

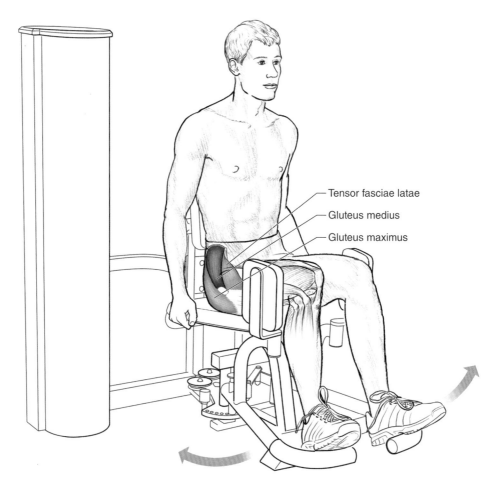

Tensor fasciae latae

Gluteus medius

Gluteus maximus

Execution

1. Sit on the abduction machine with your legs together.
2. Slowly spread your legs apart as far as possible. Keep your back flat against the pad.
3. With controlled movement, bring your legs back to the starting position.

Muscles Involved

Primary: Gluteus medius, gluteus minimus

Secondary: Gluteus maximus, piriformis, obturator externus, tensor fasciae latae

Cycling Focus

Similar to the hip adductors, the hip abductors play a key role in stabilizing your pedaling motion. Strong stabilizers will be especially helpful when you are riding with high fatigue levels—such as at the end of a race. The hip abductors are prone to spasm and cramping when you're fatigued and at the limit of your fitness. By training these muscles in the gym, you'll increase the strength of the muscle as well as the blood flow and vascular beds that course throughout the muscle. This will help prevent cramping and spasm, and it will prolong the time it takes for you to reach fatigue.

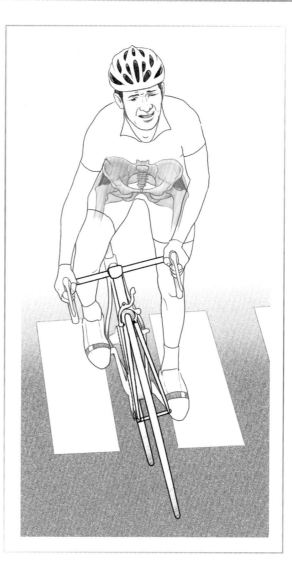

VARIATION

Fire hydrant: If you do not have access to a hip abduction machine, you can work your hip abductors using a cable-pulley system (as described in the variation of the hip adductor exercise). You can also work these muscles on the floor. The fire hydrant is a simple exercise that can be done anywhere. Position yourself on your hands and knees. Lift one leg up and out to the side, keeping your knee bent. Be sure to focus on your hip motion while lifting your leg.

Cable Back Kick

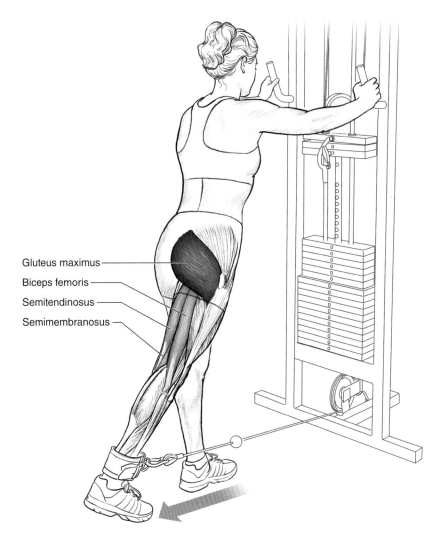

Gluteus maximus
Biceps femoris
Semitendinosus
Semimembranosus

Execution

1. Attach a low pulley to your ankle. Face the pulley system and grasp the handles.
2. Keeping your leg straight, extend at the hip, moving your foot backward.
3. Slowly return to the starting position. Complete the set and then switch sides.

Muscles Involved

Primary: Gluteus maximus

Secondary: Hamstrings

Cycling Focus

The gluteus maximus plays a huge role when you are driving the cranks on your bike. This muscle provides a large percentage of your power stroke. As you rotate over the top of your pedaling motion and start pushing down, your gluteus maximus fires to move your hip into extension. The development of this muscle is clearly visible when you look at serious cyclists. The cable back kick is fundamental to cycling training because it is the best exercise for isolating this key muscle. To save time during your workout, you can work hip adduction, hip abduction, hip extension, and hip flexion all on one side before switching the attachment to the other leg.

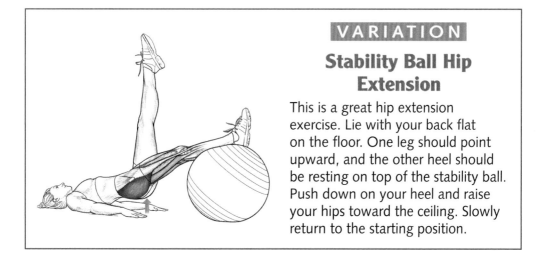

VARIATION

Stability Ball Hip Extension

This is a great hip extension exercise. Lie with your back flat on the floor. One leg should point upward, and the other heel should be resting on top of the stability ball. Push down on your heel and raise your hips toward the ceiling. Slowly return to the starting position.

Single-Leg Cable Raise

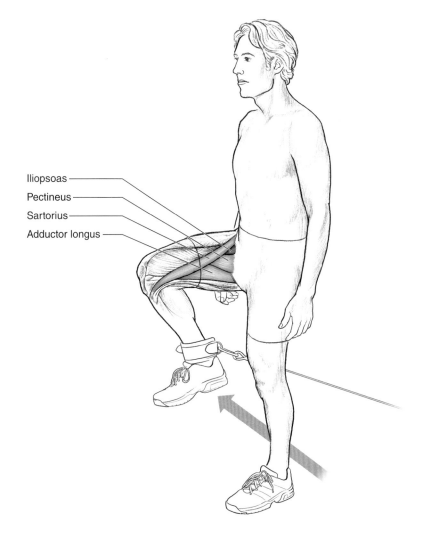

Iliopsoas
Pectineus
Sartorius
Adductor longus

Execution

1. Face away from a low pulley attached to one of your ankles. Grasp the bars for stability if necessary. Your attached leg should be in slight hip extension.
2. Pull your knee upward against the pulley resistance, bending at the hip.
3. When your thigh is parallel with the floor, slowly lower your leg back to the starting position.

Muscles Involved

Primary: Iliopsoas

Secondary: Pectineus, sartorius, adductor longus, adductor brevis

Cycling Focus

The single-leg cable raise mimics the upward drive of your leg as you rotate the cranks on your bike. Imagine surging on a climb or jumping for the line when closing on the finish. Many people talk about "pedaling in circles." They mean that you should concentrate on applying power to the pedals throughout the entire rotation of the crank. This is a good way to think about the pedaling motion, but in reality, riders pedal in more of a triangle pattern: up, down, and across the bottom. Whichever way you choose

to think about it, you should make sure that both legs continually contribute to speeding your bike forward. The single-leg cable raise will isolate the upward movement of the pedaling stroke and help train your entire pedaling "circle."

CHAPTER 8

LEGS: COMPLETE POWER

Without a doubt, the legs, hips, and buttocks are the driving force of every cyclist, and these areas of the body should be the focal point of each rider's weight training program. The previous chapters of the book focused on helping you work toward developing a strong foundation. This chapter and the next will help you use this solid base and build explosive and focused cycling power.

The exercises included here will help condition all phases of your pedal rotation. By applying power throughout the entire pedaling motion, you'll get the most efficient and consistent effort. These exercises will help tie multiple muscle groups into the same action. Whether you're in the gym or on your bike, you should focus on economy of motion. Ideally, all your effort will be contributing to increased speed and enhanced performance.

With almost any application in the real world, your muscles will be forced to work together. Imagine the movement of your legs during your pedal stroke. Depending on the exact angle of the cranks, numerous leg muscles will be firing in concert to deliver optimal power (see figure 8.1). This elegant and efficient cooperation is what makes the bicycle such a fantastic transport.

While performing the exercises in this chapter, you should focus on developing explosive power. Use the descriptions in the Cycling Focus section to hone your mental image when completing each exercise. Many

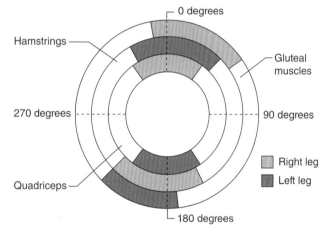

Figure 8.1   Muscle activation during the pedal stroke.
Adapted from I.E. Faria and P.R. Cavanagh, 1978, *The physiology and biomechanics of cycling* (New York: Wiley). By permission of I.E. Faria.

of the exercises will become mainstays in your weight training program because you will be impressed by the direct gains you see when riding.

Because you'll be using multiple muscle groups, you can often lift heavy weights while performing the exercises in this chapter. Be careful not to overdo it and hurt yourself. Make sure you take adequate time off between workout sessions, and always yield to any pain or discomfort in your joints, back, or muscles during the exercise.

Before beginning, make sure you are adequately warmed and stretched. As a general rule, you should perform some isolated-muscle exercises before moving to these exercises that work multiple muscle groups. This will not only warm up the muscle but will also place some fatigue on the muscle groups. Because of the induced fatigue, you'll be lifting slightly lighter weights. This will lessen the load on your supporting structures (such as your back and ligaments) and reduce the risk of injury.

Barbell Squat

Rectus femoris

Vastus lateralis

Vastus intermedius

Gluteus maximus

Biceps femoris

Gastrocnemius

Soleus

Execution

1. Stand with your feet slightly wider than your pedal width, and place the bar across your shoulders.
2. Keeping your back straight, bend at the knees until your thighs are parallel with the floor.
3. Slowly extend your knees and return to the standing position.

Muscles Involved

Primary: Gluteus maximus, quadriceps

Secondary: Erector spinae, hamstrings, gastrocnemius, soleus, hip adductors

Cycling Focus

The barbell squat is an extremely important cycling-related exercise. It develops the power and strength needed to drive your pedal stroke. Whether you're climbing or powering on the flats, you will benefit from the gains achieved in this exercise. The barbell squat works all the major muscle groups of your lower extremity and back. While lifting, imagine yourself climbing out of the saddle on your bike. The squat exercise mimics the downstroke of your pedaling motion; this is the phase in which you will generate the largest portion of your power. During the squat exercise, you should stand with your feet mimicking their position on the pedals. Your stance should be only slightly wider than the pedal spacing on your bike (known as the Q factor). Your heel-to-toe line should also mimic your natural position on the bike. For example, if you are slightly pigeon-toed when you clip in, then you should stand similarly for the exercise.

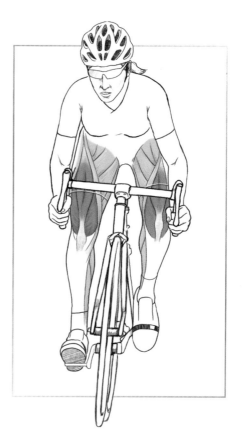

⚠ **SAFETY TIP** Because your legs and gluteals are so powerful, you'll be lifting heavy weights in the barbell squat. Good form will help prevent low back injury. Keep your spine straight and your head up during the exercise.

VARIATION

Front Squat

The front squat places increased emphasis on your quadriceps. Although you will still be training your entire lower body with this exercise, the increased work of your quadriceps prepares you to deliver optimal power over the top of your rotating pedal stroke. (Placing your heels on a small block may help with stability.)

Box Surge

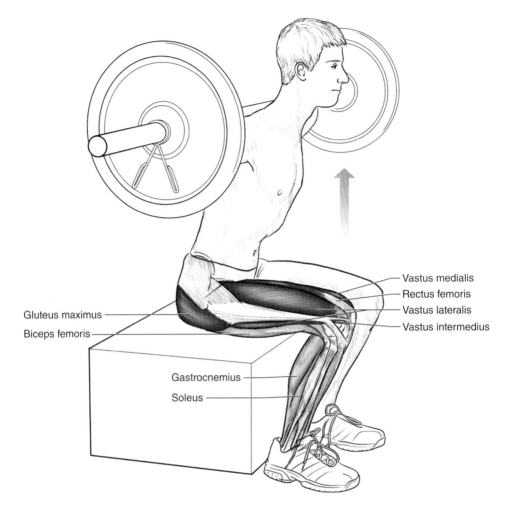

Vastus medialis
Rectus femoris
Vastus lateralis
Vastus intermedius
Gluteus maximus
Biceps femoris
Gastrocnemius
Soleus

Execution

1. Stand with your feet slightly wider than your pedal width, and place the bar across your shoulders. A box or bench should be positioned behind you.

2. Bend at the knees until you are sitting on the box. (Your knees should be bent at or just above 90 degrees when you are sitting on the box.) Disengage your leg muscles.

3. From a "dead start," slowly extend your knees and return to the standing position.

Muscles Involved

Primary: Gluteus maximus, quadriceps

Secondary: Erector spinae, hamstrings, gastrocnemius, soleus, hip adductors

Cycling Focus

This exercise helps develop raw, explosive power that will give you a strong starting snap in your pedaling downstroke—the kind of power suited to attacking a climb or covering a sudden fast break by another rider. Imagine the end of a bike race when it's just you and one other rider. The one who can get the strongest "jump" at the appropriate time will raise his arms in victory at the line. This exercise disengages your muscles while sitting on the box so you can develop maximum power at your weakest point. You must sit fully on your buttocks and relax your leg muscles. You want to lift the weight from a dead rest. This will remove the "spring" or "rebound" advantage of the traditional squat.

⚠ **SAFETY TIP** Once you sit on the box, you should use a smooth movement to stand. If you jerk or abruptly move, you may injure your back or knees.

VARIATION

Box surge on stability disks: For an extremely difficult exercise, try standing on stability disks while surging from the box. This exercise takes practice and balance, so start with a low weight and work your way up!

Split-Leg Squat

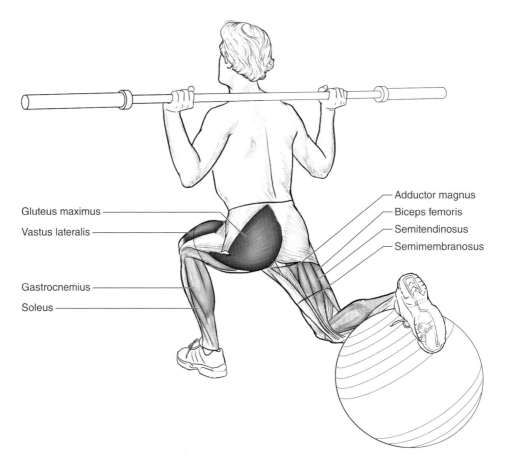

Gluteus maximus
Vastus lateralis
Gastrocnemius
Soleus

Adductor magnus
Biceps femoris
Semitendinosus
Semimembranosus

Execution

1. While standing, place a barbell over your shoulders.
2. Place one foot slightly forward. Extend your other leg back, placing your foot on top of a stability ball.
3. Slowly bend your front knee until it makes a 90-degree angle. Return to the standing position.

Muscles Involved

Primary: Gluteus maximus, quadriceps

Secondary: Erector spinae, hamstrings, gastrocnemius, soleus, hip adductors

Cycling Focus

Imagine climbing up a steep grade and having to accelerate to match an attack from another rider. You'll need to maximize your entire pedal stroke to meet the challenge. Split-leg squats will help you develop powerful quadriceps, which will enable you to deliver a strong kick over the top of your pedal stroke. This is also an important exercise for cyclists because it lets them train each leg individually. Without knowing it, cyclists often have one leg that is disproportionately stronger than the other. This can be hidden when the cyclist is performing exercises that use both legs simultaneously. In the split-leg squat, any inequalities will be recognized and can be remedied through training.

VARIATIONS

Split-leg squat with bench: For more stability, you can place your rear foot on a bench. This will help if you are finding it difficult to keep your balance while doing the exercise with a stability ball.

Smith machine split-leg squat: The Smith machine is another more stable option. Using the Smith machine will help stabilize your movement. It will also help protect your back and provide you with an artificial spotter.

Machine Leg Press

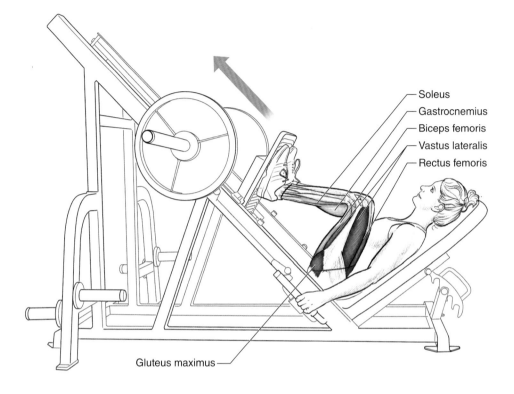

Soleus
Gastrocnemius
Biceps femoris
Vastus lateralis
Rectus femoris

Gluteus maximus

Execution

1. Sit on the sled with your feet shoulder-width apart and your back flat against the padded seat.
2. Slowly bend your knees and lower the weight until your knees are at a 90-degree angle.
3. Extend your legs and return the weight to its original position. (Don't lock your knees.)

Muscles Involved

Primary: Gluteus maximus, quadriceps

Secondary: Erector spinae, hamstrings, gastrocnemius, soleus, hip adductors

Cycling Focus

This is a cyclist's bread-and-butter leg exercise. The leg press machine allows you to work on your upward surge. It helps you develop explosive cycling power. Because of the solid back support provided by the machine, there is less chance that you'll injure yourself when accelerating out of your squat position. By changing your foot position, you can emphasize different muscles of your lower extremity. Placing your feet high on the footplate will focus the training on your gluteus maximus and hamstrings. A low foot position will emphasize your quadriceps. Stance width can also be adjusted to focus your training on various muscles. A wide stance especially works your vastus medialis (inner quad), sartorius, and hip adductors. A narrow stance puts the focus on your vastus lateralis (outer quad) and hip abductors.

VARIATION

Hack squat: While standing, position your back flat against the sliding back rest. Wedge your shoulders snugly under the pads. Slowly perform a squat as described on page 148. The hack squat places added emphasis on your quadriceps. Like the leg press, you can switch between squats, calf extensions, and reverse calf raises (described in chapter 7). You can also exercise one leg at a time to ensure equal training.

Wall Stability Ball Squat

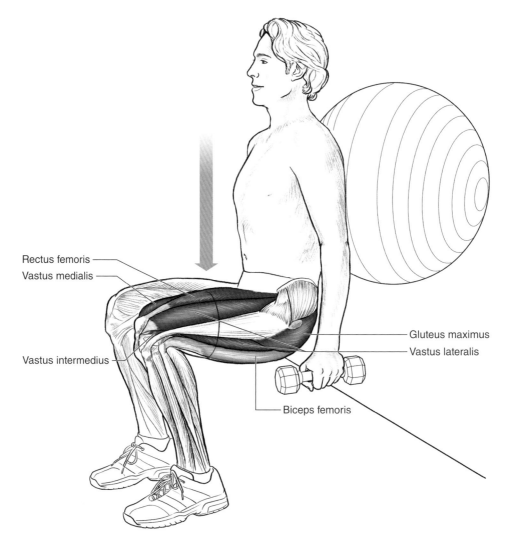

Rectus femoris
Vastus medialis
Vastus intermedius
Gluteus maximus
Vastus lateralis
Biceps femoris

Execution

1. While standing, place the stability ball between your lower back and the wall.
2. Hold two dumbbells in your hands with your arms straight at your sides.
3. Perform a squat motion, bending your knees to 90 degrees. The ball will roll as you squat.
4. Return to the starting position.

Muscles Involved

Primary: Quadriceps, gluteus maximus

Secondary: Hamstrings, hip adductors

Cycling Focus

This exercise not only helps you develop strong pistons to drive the pedals, but also emphasizes your abdominal muscles, back muscles, and lower extremity stabilizers. Because the stability ball can roll any direction on the wall, you'll be forced to control your foundation as you lift the weight. This instability helps strengthen your core and prepares you for the later miles of your rides. When you become tired, your form can start to fail, and your efficiency will drop. The longer you can prevent this from occurring, the better results you'll have.

VARIATIONS

Timed squat: Position yourself as described, but don't use the dumbbells. Rather than do repetitions, proceed to the down position and hold it for a fixed amount of time. For example, you could hold the position for 30 seconds, 1 minute, 2 minutes, or more depending on your strength and conditioning.

Squat on stability disks: For some real instability, perform the timed exercise while standing on two stability disks. This places even greater emphasis on all your accessory muscles.

Single-Leg Stability Arc

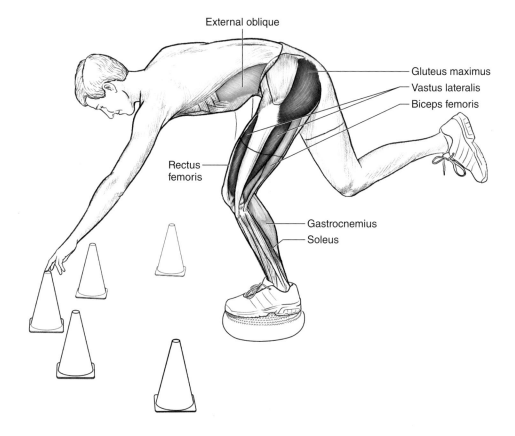

Execution

1. Place an arc of five cones in front of you, and stand with one foot on a stability disk.
2. Bend your leg and lean forward to touch one of the cones with your same-side hand.
3. Return to the standing position and repeat the movement to each of the cones.

Muscles Involved

Primary: Gluteus maximus, quadriceps

Secondary: Erector spinae, hamstrings, gastrocnemius, soleus, hip adductors, rectus abdominis, accessory stabilizers

Cycling Focus

The single-leg stability arc places a large amount of strain on all the primary and accessory muscles used in cycling. This exercise may look simple at first glance, but if you do it correctly, it will be very taxing. Many professional cyclists use this exercise early in the season to help prepare them for the many miles that lie ahead. Time after time, I've seen athletes with mid- and late-season injuries because their foundation was not able to handle the season's load. This exercise establishes your base. Because it is such a fundamental movement and

relies so heavily on all your stabilizers, it conditions not only your muscles, but also your joints, tendons, and ligaments. During a hard ride, when fatigue is maximal, you can start to lose your pedaling form. This exercise trains you to maintain proper motion when your primary muscles (quadriceps, hamstrings, gluteals) are nearly spent.

VARIATIONS

Dumbbell stability arc: Holding a dumbbell during the exercise will increase the difficulty level and place even greater strain on your accessory muscles.

Floor stability arc: If you have trouble maintaining your balance on the stability disk, you can start with your foot on the floor and work up to using the disk over time.

Double-Leg Power Jump

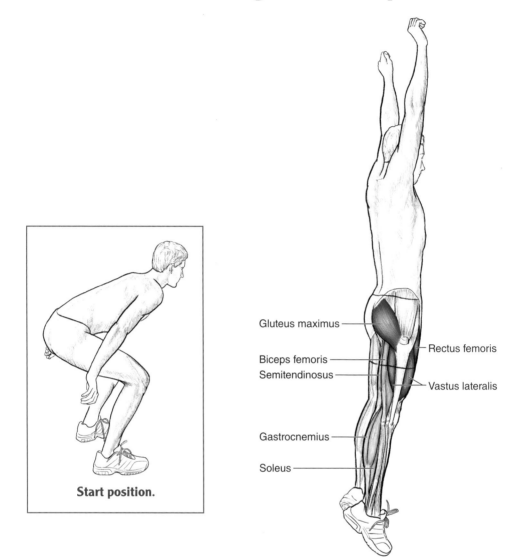

Start position.

Gluteus maximus

Rectus femoris

Biceps femoris

Semitendinosus

Vastus lateralis

Gastrocnemius

Soleus

Execution

1. Stand in the squat position with your feet slightly wider than shoulder-width apart. Your knees should be at 90 degrees.
2. Aggressively throw your arms forward and upward while jumping as high and as far forward as possible.
3. Upon landing, return to the squatting position and repeat.

Muscles Involved

Primary: Gluteus maximus, quadriceps

Secondary: Erector spinae, hamstrings, gastrocnemius, soleus, hip adductors

Cycling Focus

This exercise is all about explosive cycling power. Many professional cyclists use this simple exercise to develop sudden, high-end power. The power jump helps you build the strength to sprint for the line or to break away on a climb. Think of yourself as a coiled spring, and start the exercise with an explosive burst. Be sure you don't do this exercise when your muscles are cold (this could result in a pulled muscle). After the aggressive upward phase, you should try to land as gently as possible. This forces all your muscles to activate once again, and you get the most benefit from your training.

VARIATION

Single-leg jump: Perform the jump the same as the double-leg version, but keep one foot off the floor the entire time. These jumps are difficult but will further develop your explosive power.

Lunge

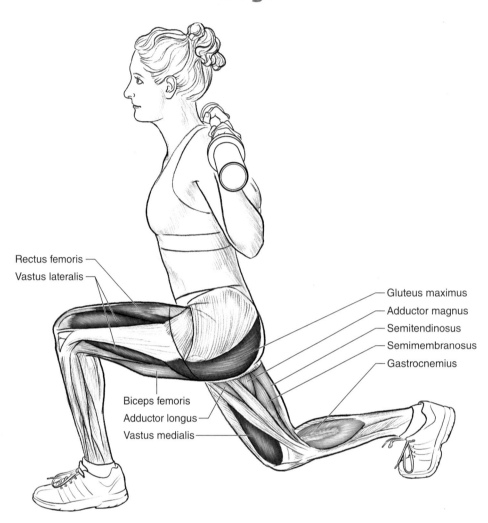

Rectus femoris
Vastus lateralis

Gluteus maximus
Adductor magnus
Semitendinosus
Semimembranosus
Gastrocnemius

Biceps femoris
Adductor longus
Vastus medialis

Execution

1. Stand with your feet shoulder-width apart and with the barbell over your shoulders.

2. Keeping your back straight and your head up, step forward until your front knee is making a 90-degree angle and your front thigh is parallel with the floor. Your trailing knee will be slightly above the ground. To avoid injury, make sure your knee does not move forward beyond your toes.

3. Return to the starting position by stepping back with your forward foot. Repeat the exercise with your opposite leg.

Muscles Involved

Primary: Gluteus maximus, quadriceps

Secondary: Erector spinae, hamstrings, gastrocnemius, soleus, hip adductors

Cycling Focus

When you see a professional cyclist zip by in his tucked aero position during a time trial, you can see the raw power in his legs as he taps out his cadence. The lunge exercise brings you that same power. This exercise not only develops power for your downstroke, but also for your upstroke, giving you a consistent pedaling motion. Most professionals recognize the importance of this exercise and include it in their training program. You'll definitely feel this workout the next day, so don't overdo it in the gym. You may have a tendency to lean forward as you become more fatigued; you must focus on keeping your back straight throughout the exercise.

⚠ **SAFETY TIP** Make certain to keep your head up. This helps keep your spine straight and protects your back.

VARIATION

Side Lunge

The lateral lunge develops strength through your legs' entire range of motion. By training this lateral movement, you'll stabilize your knee joint and prevent injury.

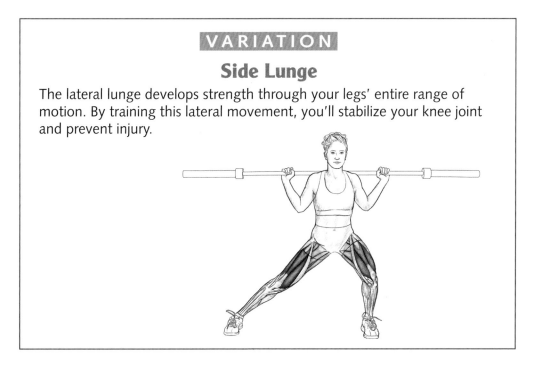

Step-Up

Rectus femoris
Vastus lateralis
Gastrocnemius
Biceps femoris
Gluteus maximus

Finish position.

Execution

1. Facing a 16- to 18-inch (41 to 46 cm) box, stand with the barbell over your shoulders.

2. Step up with your left leg. Follow through with your right leg until your left leg is straight and your right thigh is parallel with the ground. (Your right leg never touches the box.)

3. Step back down with your right foot first, followed by your left foot. After you complete a set, repeat on the opposite side.

Muscles Involved

Primary: Gluteus maximus, quadriceps

Secondary: Erector spinae, hamstrings, gastrocnemius, soleus, hip adductors

Cycling Focus

Climbing ability is fundamental to every cyclist. When you work this exercise in the gym, imagine attacking the peloton on a long climb. With each dynamic step upward during the exercise, you'll mimic your powerful pedaling downstroke. Controlling your body as you step up helps strengthen your primary force muscles and also conditions your back muscles, abdominal muscles, and accessory leg muscles. Whether you're climbing in or out of the saddle on your bike, the extension of your gluteus maximus and quadriceps plays a major role in power transfer to the bike. By using the step-up exercise, you'll definitely see returns in your climbing prowess.

VARIATION

Side Step-Up

You can perform this same exercise to the side. (You may need a slightly lower box to perform this exercise.) Standing with the box to your right, step up with your right leg while keeping your back straight. Follow through with your left leg until your left thigh is parallel with the floor. Return your left foot to the floor.

CHAPTER 9

WHOLE-BODY TRAINING FOR CYCLING

The exercises in this chapter are the most engaging of the entire book. The previous chapters all focused on various parts of your body—arms, back, legs, and so on. Even though chapter 8 provided exercises for working multiple leg muscles together, the focus was always on the lower extremity. This chapter provides exercises for training multiple muscle groups simultaneously, combining both upper and lower body movements. You'll be focusing on total-body fitness, flexibility, and strength. Not only will you be gaining muscle strength and increased power, but because you'll be using so many different muscles simultaneously, you will also be gaining excellent cardiorespiratory fitness. Certainly, this is my favorite chapter of the book, and I always try to include some of these exercises in my workouts.

As previously mentioned, one of my fundamental training principles is that people must use their workouts efficiently and effectively. With the exercises in this chapter, you will be making good use of the time you spend in the gym. By combining various movements into one exercise, you will simultaneously train many of the key cycling muscles. With oxygen and blood flow in higher demand, your body will have to become more adept at utilizing the scarce resources. Distribution of fuel and removal of muscle by-products will force your entire system to work more efficiently.

These combined exercises are not only multidimensional but also interesting and entertaining to perform. Keeping your mind fresh and motivated can become a chore as the season progresses. Hopefully these exercises will help keep you fired up for your gym workouts. Remember that if you start to feel bored with your routines, you need to change things. Just going through the motions will surely limit the potential gains of your workout.

Coordinated Training: Muscles Working Together

Although it is important to train each muscle in isolation, as stated previously, it is also fundamental that you train multiple muscle groups in unison. When you are riding your bike, your body will be in a dynamic state. You'll never be relying on just one muscle or muscle group. Your body works as an entire coordinated system. The whole-body exercises will help you train for this concerted effort and prepare you for the stressors of the road. After focusing on these exercises in your training, you'll definitely see improved performance while riding.

To perform the fluid movements of these exercises, you must rely on your solid base and core while using the full mobility of your arms and legs. With every extension, twist, and flexion, you'll be training not only the muscles working against the resistance, but also the dynamic stabilizers and movement antagonists. These are the muscles that are vitally important when you are fatigued and hitting your maximal effort on the bike. When you leave the gym, you'll feel as if you've been worked over—and that's the point!

The importance of efficiency was discussed earlier in this book. Any wasted motion results in decreased performance. Since even the best cyclists are only 27 percent efficient, you can see that every little improvement in movement increases power transfer to the bike. If you want to get the most out of your pedal stroke, you need to apply force to the pedals for the entire revolution of the crank. While trying these workouts in the gym, concentrate on smooth, constant force motion. Don't jerk or cheat by bouncing or overusing your stronger muscle groups. Keep the movements uniform and consistent.

Both sides of your body work together to drive the bike forward. One side pulls on the pedal while the other side pushes. This combined effort keeps forceful tension on the chain and rear wheel. Although the power delivered to the pedals will vary through each rotation of the crank, your focus and goal should be to decrease this variation. Figure 9.1 compares the power input for a choppy pedal stroke versus a more smooth power delivery. Note that the first graph shows deep valleys between the peaks—there is a wide variation between maximal and minimal power input. The lower image shows the ideal situation. Only a small variation is shown between the maximum power and minimum power provided by each leg. While working all the exercises in this book, you should focus on performing a smooth and well-coordinated movement. Keep abrupt movements and jerks to a minimum. Think about applying a constant power input throughout the entire range of motion.

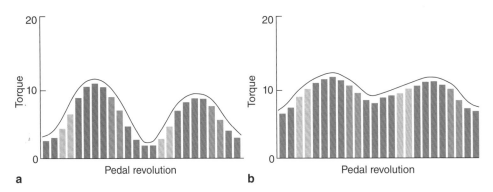

Figure 9.1   Sine curve comparing *(a)* a choppy pedal stroke caused by unequal effort by the legs and *(b)* a smooth stroke resulting from equal power delivery.
Adapted, by permission, from bar graphs generated by the CompuTrainer SpinScan™ Pedal Stroke Analyzer. Original image available at www.racermateinc.com/spinscan.asp [September 9, 2008]. SpinScan™ is a registered trademark of RacerMate, Inc.

As with all your workouts, make sure that you're properly fueled for the task. Don't skip meals prior to your workouts, and make sure you have plenty of hydration. Once finished with your training, you should try to eat within 30 minutes. The timing is important because your metabolism is revved up and the calories will be used more efficiently. Your body uses the protein consumed to rebuild the muscle damage from weightlifting, and the carbohydrates you eat will replenish depleted energy supplies.

Warm-Up and Stretching

As mentioned previously, you must warm up properly before engaging in these exercises. You will be using your entire body for these exercises, so you'll have to do some whole-body movements such as rowing or jumping rope. After a cardio warm-up and some stretching, you should perform the movements of each exercise without using weights. This loosens up all the various muscle groups and will help you focus on proper form. If you are doing multiple sets, start with a lighter weight and then increase the weight for successive sets. This gives your muscles more time to warm up to the challenge of the workout. These exercises are very taxing, so cutting corners in the warm-up could lead to injury. Remember, weight training is all about building on previous gains. Slow and steady wins the race. Injuring yourself in the gym is totally demoralizing, especially since proper warm-up and graded effort can alleviate much of the possibility of hurting yourself.

Goalies

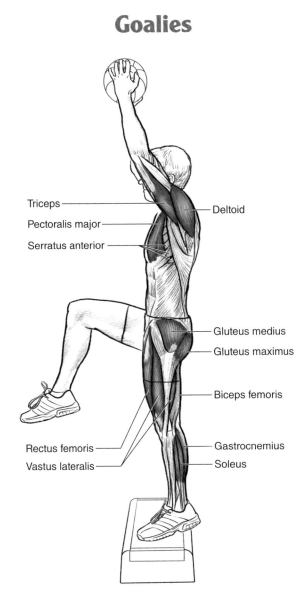

Triceps
Pectoralis major
Serratus anterior

Deltoid

Gluteus medius
Gluteus maximus

Biceps femoris

Rectus femoris
Vastus lateralis

Gastrocnemius
Soleus

Execution

1. Holding a medicine ball at your chest, stand in front of a platform.
2. With a forceful movement, step onto the platform. Drive your non-weight-bearing knee upward while extending your support leg. Simultaneously extend both your arms above your head. When finished, you should be standing on your tiptoes (on one leg) and holding the medicine ball over your head.
3. With controlled movement, step backward off the platform and return to your starting position.
4. Alternate your step-up leg.

Muscles Involved

Primary: Quadriceps, gluteus maximus, gluteus medius, gluteus minimus, gastrocnemius, soleus, deltoid, triceps, pectoralis major

Secondary: Hamstrings, erector spinae, trapezius, serratus anterior

Cycling Focus

This exercise trains you to maintain your form while putting in a hard effort. When you step up and thrust the medicine ball above your head, all your stabilizer muscles fire. Because you're standing on only one leg while holding a load over your head, your pelvis must lock into position. This is similar to putting in a hard effort while riding. Whether you're seated or standing on the bike, your pelvis must provide a solid foundation to counteract the different actions of each of your legs. Because goalies involve the added effort of your torso and upper extremities, you'll also be training for the many hours of supporting your body weight over the handlebars.

VARIATION

Stairs and press: If you have access to stairs in an arena or stadium, this is an excellent alternative to goalies. Hold a dumbbell in each hand. Skip every other step as you ascend the stairs. While climbing, perform an arm press with each dumbbell above your head. You can do this with both arms together or arms alternating.

Deadlift With Push-Up

Start position.

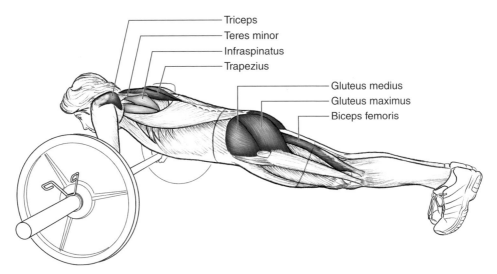

Triceps
Teres minor
Infraspinatus
Trapezius
Gluteus medius
Gluteus maximus
Biceps femoris

Execution

1. With the barbell on the floor, squat down and grasp the bar with a palm-down grip. Your shins should be touching the bar.
2. Straighten to the upright position. The barbell should slide up your shins and then your thighs.
3. Lower the barbell back to the starting position.
4. Jump back with both feet so you are in the push-up position.
5. Perform a push-up, jump to the starting position, and repeat the entire cycle. Never release your grip on the bar.

Muscles Involved

Primary: Hamstrings, gluteus maximus, gluteus medius, gluteus minimus, trapezius, triceps, pectoralis major

Secondary: Erector spinae, deltoid, supraspinatus, infraspinatus, teres minor, rectus abdomini

Cycling Focus

This exercise prepares your body for the load of cycling training. Because of the standard bent-over position that you assume on your bike, riding places extreme pressure on the entire back side of your body (from your neck down to your calves). A difficult workout or race only multiplies this stress. At the end of a long climb, you'll note the strain of your neck, back, and hamstrings—all the muscles trained by this combination exercise.

The deadlift with push-up will also condition your arms and prepare them for supporting the load of your body when you are in the riding position. Make sure you don't use a weight that is too heavy. The exercise may seem easy for the first couple repetitions, but the difficulty will increase exponentially as you approach the end of the set. You'll really feel the effects of this exercise the next day after training; take care that you don't overdo it.

Medicine Ball Throw

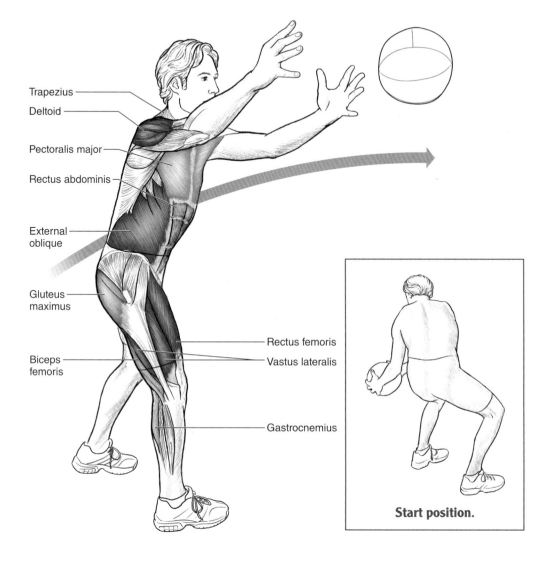

Trapezius
Deltoid
Pectoralis major
Rectus abdominis
External oblique
Gluteus maximus
Biceps femoris
Rectus femoris
Vastus lateralis
Gastrocnemius

Start position.

Execution

1. Hold a medicine ball in both hands, and stand about 8 to 10 feet (2.4 to 3.0 m) in front of a wall.
2. Twist your trunk and bring the ball back to one side. You should stand with one foot slightly ahead of the other.
3. With an explosive movement, heave the ball at the wall.
4. Catch the ball after it bounces off the wall and rapidly repeat the action on the opposite side. Continue alternating until you finish the set.

Muscles Involved

Primary: External oblique, internal oblique, rectus abdominis, deltoid, quadriceps

Secondary: Biceps, trapezius, pectoralis major, gluteus maximus, hamstrings, gastrocnemius, soleus

Cycling Focus

Cycling is all about surges. A surge at the right time can create a gap that may give you the opportunity to win the race. Imagine being on your bike and climbing with your competitors. You decide the time is now, and you make an explosive jump. After your acceleration, you're able to hold the speed for two minutes. Slowly, you back off and return to your previous pace. Although you may be climbing at the same speed as your competitors, you've got yourself a significant gap. Now you can try to hold it to the finish. The medicine ball throw will help you develop the explosive surge needed in order to make this kind of successful race move. Focus on the explosive nature of the throw. The word *heave* accurately describes what you need to do in this exercise. Throw that ball with all your might!

VARIATION

Squat with front throw: Start in a squat position while you hold a medicine ball at your chest. Surge to the standing position. At the same time, throw the ball at the wall in front of you. (Use a pushing motion on the ball, as if you're making a basketball pass.) Return to the starting position and repeat the action in rapid succession. To mix it up even further, you can perform the same exercise but throw the medicine ball forward from behind your head. The motion is similar to throwing a soccer ball over your head.

Lunge With Biceps Curl

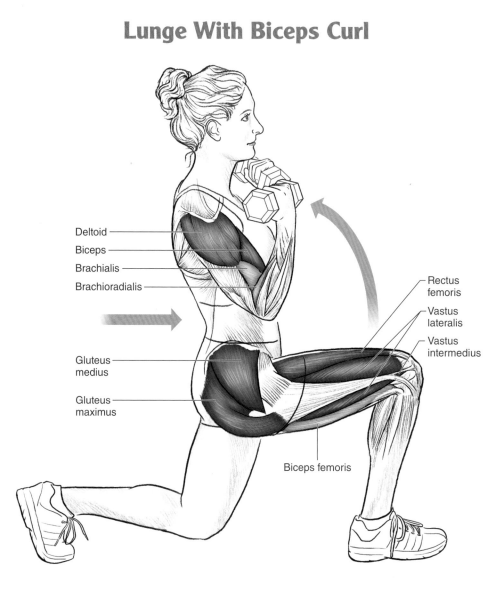

Deltoid

Biceps

Brachialis

Brachioradialis

Rectus femoris

Vastus lateralis

Vastus intermedius

Gluteus medius

Gluteus maximus

Biceps femoris

Execution

1. Stand erect with a dumbbell in each hand.
2. Perform a lunge, stepping forward with one leg.
3. While in the lunge position, perform a curl with both arms simultaneously.
4. Reverse the steps and repeat with the opposite leg.

Muscles Involved

Primary: Quadriceps, gluteus maximus, gluteus medius, gluteus minimus, deltoid, biceps

Secondary: Hamstrings, brachialis, brachioradialis, forearms

Cycling Focus

The next time you attack while riding, note the downward force of each pedal stroke. Also feel your biceps pulling up on the bars as you stand to deliver maximum power with your legs. Throughout your entire acceleration, you'll need a strong foundation— from your chest to your pelvis—to provide support as you drive your legs through their rotation. The lunge with biceps curl combines a primary exercise used in cycling training—the lunge—with an exercise for strengthening the core and arms. With this combination exercise, you'll definitely be getting a lot of work in a limited time.

VARIATION

Side Lunge With Shrug

Hold a dumbbell in each hand. Perform a side lunge by stepping out to the side with one leg. While in the downward position, shrug with the dumbbells. Return to the starting position and repeat the action on the other side.

Woodchopper

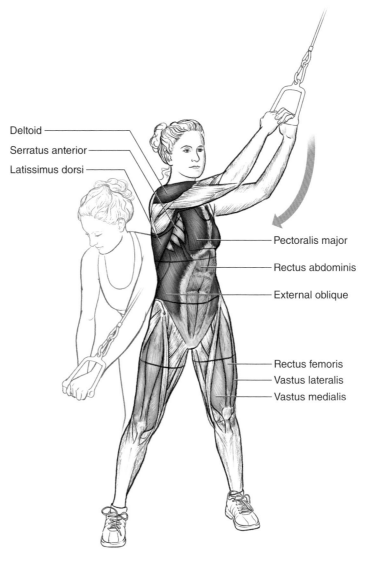

Deltoid

Serratus anterior

Latissimus dorsi

Pectoralis major

Rectus abdominis

External oblique

Rectus femoris

Vastus lateralis

Vastus medialis

Execution

1. Stand sideways next to a high pulley and grasp the handle with both hands. Your arms should be extended above your head and off to the same side as the pulley.

2. Start by pulling your arms downward. As your hands pass your shoulders, begin to twist and crunch your abdomen. Continue pulling downward as you flex your knees into the squat position.

3. You should finish the movement with your knees bent, your trunk twisted, your abdominal muscles crunched, and your arms extended downward to the opposite side of where you started.

4. Using controlled movement, return to the starting position.

Muscles Involved

Primary: Rectus abdominis, external oblique, internal oblique, latissimus dorsi, deltoid, pectoralis major

Secondary: Quadriceps, gluteus maximus, gluteus medius, gluteus minimus, teres major, serratus anterior

Cycling Focus

As discussed in the chapter about training the abdomen, cyclists need to ensure that they have adequate core conditioning. Because you will spend so much time bent forward on your bike, your back strength can overwhelm your abdominal muscles. This may lead to knee, hip, or back pain. The woodchopper exercise is very effective because it works most of your anterior (front-side) muscles. I'm a big fan of cable and pulley systems. These systems allow you to quickly change from one exercise to another, and they provide minimal stabilization while you are performing a movement. Remember, any instability during motion will force your body to work harder and train all the stabilizing muscles.

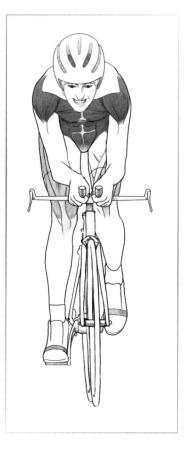

Reverse Woodchopper

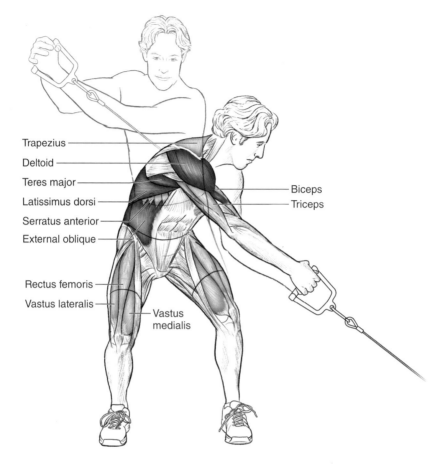

Trapezius
Deltoid
Teres major
Latissimus dorsi
Serratus anterior
External oblique
Rectus femoris
Vastus lateralis
Vastus medialis
Biceps
Triceps

Execution

1. Stand sideways to a low pulley and grasp the handle with both hands. Your arms should be extended toward the ground and to the same side as the pulley. You should be bent over and twisted to the side of the pulley.

2. Start by pulling your arms upward. As your hands cross knee level, begin to straighten and untwist your abdomen. Continue pulling upward as you extend your knees.

3. You should finish the movement with your knees extended and your torso straight and upright. Your arms should be extended upward to the opposite side from where you started.

4. Using controlled movement, return to the starting position.

Muscles Involved

Primary: Latissimus dorsi, external oblique, internal oblique, deltoid, teres major

Secondary: Quadriceps, gluteus maximus, gluteus medius, gluteus minimus, trapezius, rhomboid, triceps, serratus anterior, biceps

Cycling Focus

Although this exercise seems similar to the standard woodchopper, it works a different group of muscles. Whereas the standard woodchopper works the front of the body, the reverse woodchopper works the back of the body. As discussed, cyclists develop strong back muscles. The reverse woodchopper will help you build the fitness and strength that your legs, back, and arms need in order to sustain power for long periods of time. During this exercise, you should work on exploding from the starting position.

⚠ **SAFETY TIP** Be sure to warm up and limit the weight used. It is easy to hurt yourself when powerfully uncoiling your body in this exercise.

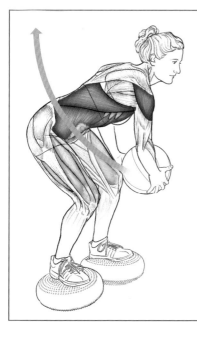

VARIATION

Medicine Ball Reverse Woodchopper

You can perform the same exercise with the medicine ball. Instead of using a pulley system, hold a medicine ball low and off to one side. With a surge of power, raise the ball upward and across your body until the ball is above your shoulder on the opposite side. Imagine uncoiling a spring as your body moves the ball from the starting position to the finish. You can also stand on stability disks to increase the difficulty.

Squat Press

Start position.

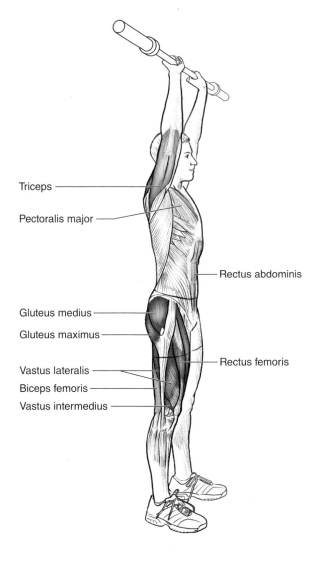

Triceps

Pectoralis major

Rectus abdominis

Gluteus medius

Gluteus maximus

Rectus femoris

Vastus lateralis

Biceps femoris

Vastus intermedius

Execution

1. Hold a barbell across your chest with a palm-out grip. Start in the squatting position.
2. Extend at the knees and bring yourself to an erect position.
3. Push the barbell upward, performing a shoulder press.
4. Reverse the two separate motions to return to the starting position.

Muscles Involved

Primary: Quadriceps, gluteus maximus, gluteus medius, gluteus minimus, anterior deltoid, triceps

Secondary: Hamstrings, hip adductors, erector spinae, rectus abdominis, trapezius, upper pectoralis major

Cycling Focus

Perform this exercise with some gusto! Make sure you're warmed up and that your form is correct—but then let it rip. The idea is to develop explosive power. You can also work on your endurance by doing increased repetitions. The squat press helps you build the type of power and endurance you'll need when you attack your competitors on a climb. As you stand to surge on your bike, you need to put a small gap between you and your rivals. This prevents your competition from getting a free tow up the road. Once you have a gap, dig deep and try to free yourself from the frantic chase behind.

⚠ **SAFETY TIP** The importance of keeping your back straight during this exercise cannot be overstated. Throughout the movement, you should keep your chin up and focus on your form. As you tire, you'll be tempted to "cheat" on the movement. Doing so can lead to undue stress and can result in injury.

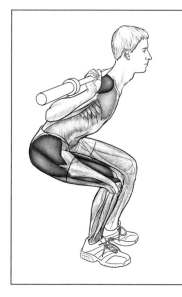

VARIATION

Behind-the-Head Squat Press

Perform the same exercise as described, but start with the barbell behind your head. After standing from the squat position, press the bar over your head.

Floor Wiper

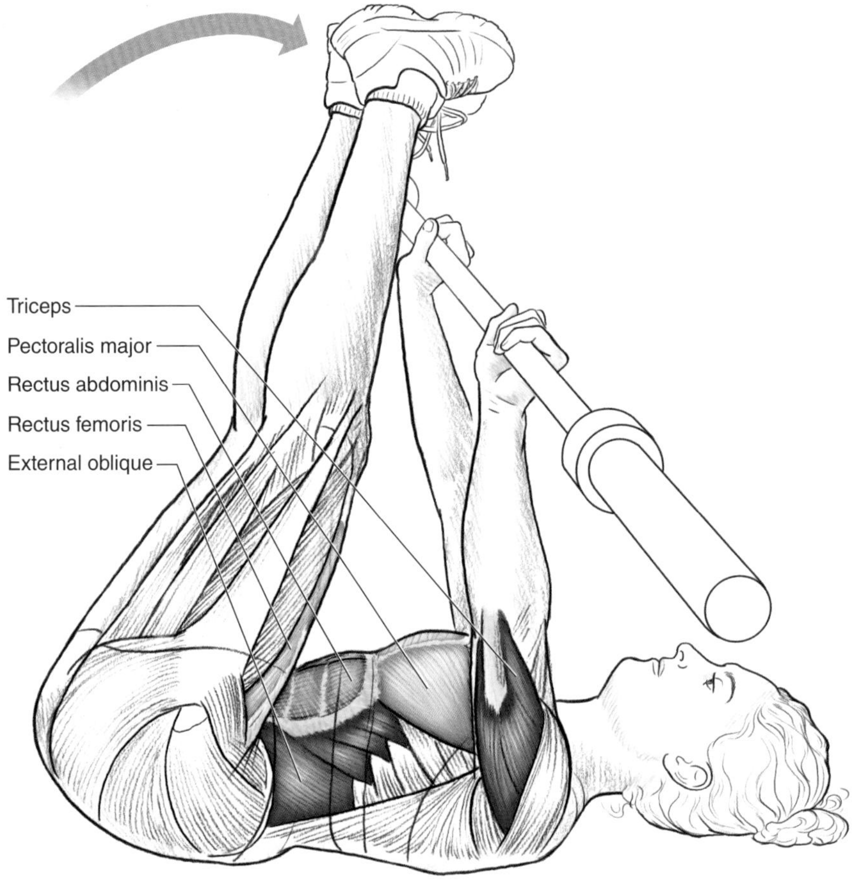

Triceps
Pectoralis major
Rectus abdominis
Rectus femoris
External oblique

Execution

1. Lie flat on your back on the floor. Hold a barbell with your arms extended above your chest.
2. Keeping the barbell stationary, perform a straight leg lift, bringing both feet toward one end of the barbell.
3. Lower your feet back to the floor.
4. Repeat the exercise, bringing your feet to the opposite side. (The barbell remains stationary for the entire set.)

Muscles Involved

Primary: Rectus abdominis, external oblique, internal oblique, triceps

Secondary: Iliopsoas, pectineus, sartorius, rectus femoris, pectoralis major

Cycling Focus

The floor wiper exercise conditions all your fundamental core muscles. These are the muscles that provide a solid base for your efforts on the bike. As mentioned, to apply proper power to the cranks, your lower extremities rely on the support of the rest of your body. Be mentally prepared for this exercise—it's tough! Floor wipers simultaneously limit your ability to breathe and condition both your large and small core muscles. You'll not only be improving your power, but also your ability to ventilate during extremely hard efforts such as a sprint or a steep climb.

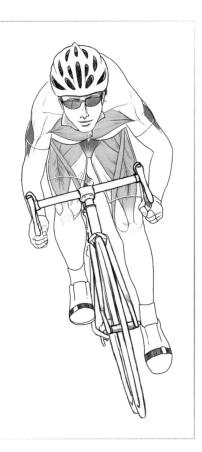

VARIATION

Dumbbell floor wiper: Instead of using a barbell, you can place a dumbbell in each hand. Keep your arms stationary and your elbows extended. Perform the leg lift from side to side as described.

Kettlebell Swing

Trapezius

Gluteus medius

Deltoid

Gluteus maximus

Rectus femoris

Biceps femoris

Vastus lateralis

Vastus intermedius

Finish position.

Execution

1. In a squat position with your feet shoulder-width apart, grasp a kettlebell resting on the floor between your legs.
2. Using primarily your lower body, surge to an erect stance while swinging the kettlebell out in front of you.
3. Keeping your arms straight, bring the kettlebell to just above shoulder height.
4. Let the kettlebell swing back down between your legs, ending in the starting position.

Muscles Involved

Primary: Quadriceps, gluteus maximus, gluteus medius, gluteus minimus, erector spinae, deltoid, rectus abdominis

Secondary: Hip adductors, hamstrings, trapezius, pectoralis major, forearms (grip strength)

Cycling Focus

When you sprint for the finish at the end of a race, your body screams in pain. You give your maximal effort to propel your bike forward as fast as possible. The kettlebell swing, like many of the other exercises in this chapter, helps you train for your maximal power output. The key moments in cycling—sprinting, attacking on a climb, and establishing a breakaway—all require explosive power, and this exercise prepares you for these tremendous efforts. While in the gym, remember

to surge from the lower extremities. This force will help bring the kettlebell upward toward your shoulders.

⚠ **SAFETY TIP** Many athletes have a tendency to lean forward during the kettlebell swing. You should focus on keeping your back straight. As you swing the kettlebell upward, try to keep your torso as stable and vertical as possible.

VARIATION

Single-Arm Kettlebell Swing

Perform the same exercise while holding the kettlebell with only one hand. You should use a lighter kettlebell for this variation. The asymmetry of the exercise will enhance the training of all your core stabilizers.

EXERCISE FINDER

ARMS

SHOULDERS AND NECK

CHEST

BACK

ABDOMEN

LEGS

WHOLE BODY

ABOUT THE AUTHOR

Photo by DeLanda Licata

Shannon Sovndal, MD, is the owner and founder of Thrive Health and Fitness Medicine (Thrive HFM), an elite team of physicians, exercise physiologists, and athletes who provide clients with the highest level of personalized health care, life management, and fitness training. Most recently, he serves as a team physician for the Garmin/Chipotle professional cycling team. He also works as a board-certified emergency medicine physician at Boulder Community Hospital in Colorado and as a physician at the General Clinical Research Center at the University of Colorado. Before becoming a physician, Sovndal raced road bikes in the United States, winning the California/Nevada District Championship and many other road races and criteriums.

Sovndal is a coauthor of *Fitness Cycling* and has written numerous sports-related articles and lectured on exercise-related topics. He attended medical school at Columbia University in New York, completed his residency at Stanford University in California, and now lives in Boulder, Colorado.